Set-Apart
Femininity

Leslie Ludy

HARVEST HOUSE PUBLISHERS
EUGENE, OREGON

Cover by Abris, Veneta, Oregon

Leslie Ludy: Published in association with Loyal Arts Literary Agency, LoyalArts.com.

SET-APART FEMININITY
Copyright © 2008 by Winston and Brooks, Inc.
Published by Harvest House Publishers
Eugene, Oregon 97402
www.harvesthousepublishers.com

Library of Congress Cataloging-in-Publication Data

Ludy, Leslie.
Set-apart femininity / Leslie Ludy.
    p. cm.
ISBN 978-0-7369-2286-9 (pbk.)
ISBN 978-0-7369-3438-1 (eBook)
1. Young women—Religious life. 2. Femininity—Religious aspects—Christianity. I. Title.
BV4551.3.L85 2008
248.8'43—dc22
                                                                                        2008002135

Printed in the United States of America

14 15 16 17 18 / VP-NI / 12 11 10 9 8

Contents

My Hope and Prayer

A few years ago, when I sat down to write my book *Authentic Beauty: The Shaping of a Set-Apart Young Woman,* I imagined myself sitting across from my reader in a quaint coffee shop for an intimate, personal conversation. I candidly shared my story, my heart, and my passion in the pages of that book. I have been so incredibly blessed that so many young women have responded to *Authentic Beauty*'s message. (In fact, a nationwide community of Christ-seeking young women has formed as a result of that book, which you can learn more about at my website, www.setapartgirl.com.) In the years since *Authentic Beauty*'s release, I have personally witnessed countless young women's hunger for the kind of femininity that counts. And that hunger has been my inspiration for this new book.

Though *Set-Apart Femininity* is written in a personal style like *Authentic Beauty* and I am honest and vulnerable in these pages, this book is not so much an intimate coffee shop conversation as it is a rousing call to arms—kind of like me standing *on top* of the table in the coffee shop and passionately proclaiming truth to any who will listen! God has challenged me in these past few years, at a much greater level than I would have thought possible, to rise above the typical mediocrity of modern-day womanhood and walk a road that is narrow, rocky, and misunderstood by the masses. *Set-Apart Femininity* presents that very same challenge to you. If you want to remain comfortably where you are in your feminine journey, this book probably won't be your cup of tea (or coffee, since we are in a coffee shop). But if you are one of the thousands of young women who hunger to showcase something spectacular and triumphant through your femininity, this book was written for you.

This is the eleventh book I have written, and it is by far the most straightforward. Even though *Authentic Beauty* was extremely candid in describing the decline of femininity in today's culture, *Set-Apart Femininity* presents spiritual challenges in a blunt, pull-no-punches way that is uncommon in today's soft-spoken Christian world. It may not sit well with those who dislike strong statements about absolute truth. It may annoy those who feel that the Bible should not be taken quite so literally. But I make no apologies for speaking this message as confidently as I believe it. Because the truths I share in this book have personally transformed my life. They have set me free. They have given me the joy, hope, and abundant life that millions of women around the world desperately seek every day. And it is my deep hope and prayer that they will do the same for you.

For resources that will help you take this message even deeper and to connect with other young women on the set-apart path, I would encourage you to visit www.setapartgirl.com. Please know that even though we may never have a chance to meet this side of heaven, I am cheering you on. I believe that God has an incredible design and purpose for your life and that, as you yield your existence to Him, your femininity truly will change this world for eternity.

Sacred Intent

unlocking femininity's spectacular purpose

1

It happened when I was 14.

Somewhere between encountering the sultry Victoria's Secret model in a push-up bra and thong and reading the "Total Body Makeover" article (complete with a three-page bikini shopping guide) in the new issue of my favorite magazine, I made the decision. Somewhere between watching a beautiful young pop star swivel-hip on stage as thousands of guys lustfully cheered and living vicariously through a perfectly proportioned actress as she found true love with a hot guy in the latest romantic comedy, I decided what I wanted to become…an alluring young woman.

It's not that I wanted to be seen as trashy or loose. But I wanted to be beautiful enough that guys would drool over me. I wanted to be the kind of girl who looked incredible in a swimsuit—the kind of girl who somehow achieved flawless skin, perfect hair, pouty lips, and dazzling white teeth while shrugging the whole thing off with an "I know I'm gorgeous but I don't really care" attitude.

It was more than just having the right look. I also needed an alluring personality. I wanted to be the kind of girl who could playfully tease cute guys just enough to toy with their desires and keep them constantly interested in me. I wanted to be the kind of girl who exuded the witty humor and endearing charm of a TV sitcom character—the kind of girl who was completely self-assured and self-confident in every situation.

I knew I had a long way to go to achieve my dream.

Back in sixth grade, I had been informed—rather rudely—by Sean Wyatt, the unofficial kingpin of Crestview Elementary, that I was (and I quote) "the sickest, most disgusting-looking girl I've ever seen!" Sean had then climbed up on the orange cafeteria table and danced around, scratching his underarms and screeching like a monkey as he pointed at me and announced to everyone present that: "She's so ugly, she belongs in a zoo!"

Sean's crowd of followers had snorted with laughter and joined in with even more creative put-downs like "You were so ugly when you were born that your mom tried to switch you with another kid at the hospital!"

I had cried for so long that night that my parents had resorted to the only thing that could possibly cheer me up—a strawberry milkshake from McDonald's.

Though I realized Sean's comments were somewhat exaggerated, I also knew that I was no beauty. I was pale and gangly with thick glasses and crooked teeth and frizzy hair and heavy black eyebrows that looked like they wanted to overtake my entire face. My clothes were never cool (I wanted Guess jeans, but my mom made me wear Lee's, which I was convinced were the source of most of my sixth-grade woes.) And I was awkward and uncomfortable around people—especially around guys. So it's no wonder that I became an easy target for Sean in his theater of cruelty.

His mocking words—along with the disdain of many other guys growing up—convinced me that I was ugly and worthless. And it created a pain inside of me that was almost too intense to bear.

Over the next few years, I worked hard to discard the label of "undesirable."

I chucked my glasses in exchange for contacts. I started wearing makeup—reasoning that if my eyelids were neon blue, maybe people wouldn't notice my too-thick eyebrows or crooked teeth. I bought the skimpiest clothes I could get past my parents. (At times I would leave the house in baggy sweats to conceal the miniskirt and halter top I was wearing underneath—the sweats came off once I got to school.) I spent countless hours wrestling with my hair, marveling at the many wonders of aerosol hairspray. I took Victoria's advice and started wearing slinky underwear and push-up bras. I stopped eating French fries because I was worried my thighs were getting fat.

And even though all of my efforts did eventually attract some approving attention from guys and put me into a more popular category at school, by the age of 14 I realized I still didn't possess the kind of allure that the world would truly applaud. I started to wonder if I ever would.

I wasn't confident and witty like the star of my favorite TV show. I didn't look like the chic and bronzed-skinned bikini model on the cover of my favorite magazine. I couldn't belt out tunes about the agony of love while lying seductively on the sand in a sexy music video like my favorite female pop star. And when the love of my life, Brandon, dumped me for a prettier girl after I'd given him my heart, the long list of everything I lacked mercilessly slapped me in the face even harder.

To become the kind of young woman that men desired and the world exalted seemed almost like an unattainable dream. But it also seemed that if I ever *could* achieve that standard, I would finally be fulfilled, secure, and happy. I would finally be truly loved and desired by the opposite sex. I would finally see my dreams come true—if I could only become that kind of beautiful, confident young woman that seemed to be everywhere but in the mirror.

As I journeyed through my young adult years, I found that there were many places I could go for help and advice in my pursuit of becoming alluring. Trendy clothing stores lured me in their doors with posters of doe-eyed, effortlessly gorgeous young women who also happened to be wearing the latest fashions hanging on the racks inside. Eye-catching magazines beckoned me to open them with bold article titles such as "Best-Kept Secrets to Becoming Sexy!" and "How to Win ANY Guy!" and "Get Your Best Body in Three Easy Steps!" Movie stars demonstrated the art of seduction as they flirted and teased and conquered men's hearts on the big screen. Popular singers taught me all about the mysteries of love and attraction through their angst-ridden tunes.

The more I listened to the incessant voice of pop culture, the more I pursued their standard for feminine beauty and appeal. I threw myself into one passionate, romantic fling after the next, trying to model the careless behavior of sitcom characters. I flirted strategically with any cute guy in my path, trying to follow the advice of every magazine on the grocery store shelf. I dressed like the models in the store windows at the mall. I obsessed over my hair, skin, body, and wardrobe like all the TV commercials urged me to.

And yet the more I tried to make myself appealing, the farther away from perfection I felt.

Elusive Allure

Only 2 percent of women think they are beautiful according to a recent survey.[1] That reality is a little strange because beauty has never been easier to come by than it is today. The plastic surgery business is booming. Beauty products are boundless. We are surrounded by a plethora of books, magazines, and TV shows that provide us with all the secrets and techniques we need to look, act, and feel like a confident, beautiful young woman. We have all the tools we need. And most of us spend a huge portion of our time trying to make ourselves alluring.

Yet in an ironic twist, we still feel ugly. We still feel worthless. We still feel like we aren't "there" yet.

A graphic designer for a major clothing label once told me, "In real life no model really looks as perfect as what you see in clothing ads or on catalog covers. We digitally alter her photo. We remove several inches from her waist and thighs. We enhance her chest size. We air-brush her skin." The world lifts up a standard for beauty that is literally impossible to achieve in real life.

As women, the desire to be beautiful is innate. We long to be seen as attractive, appealing, and desirable. We dream of capturing the heart of a noble prince with our stunning beauty, like the princesses in our childhood fairy tales. But our longing to be loved and wooed by a heroic groom didn't originate with Cinderella—it's actually a Biblical concept. The entire Bible is a beautiful love story between Christ and His bride—drawing us, wooing us, and loving us the way we have always dreamed. Song of Solomon, for example, is just one of many beautiful portrayals of our heavenly Bridegroom tenderly pursuing His bride. Jesus is the only One who can truly satisfy the deepest desires of our hearts. And yet, most of us turn to everything *but* Him in a desperate attempt to find the approval we crave. And pop culture preys upon our longings for love like a relentless vulture. They keep dangling the carrot temptingly in front of us, urging us to spend our time, money, and energy pursuing the "next great thing" that will bring us one step closer to the dream.

And all too often we fall for it. We buy the clothes. We read the magazines. We watch the commercials. We let the moviemakers and the fashion industry and the advertising executives define who we become as young women.

Of course, many young women are a bit more subtle in their pursuit of beauty than I was at 14. Most of us don't want to admit—even to ourselves—just how consumed we are with making ourselves appealing. We come up with clever excuses and disguises for our obsessions.

Modern feminism has done its job well, reminding us that we shouldn't seek the approval of the opposite sex, convincing us that everything we do should be only for ourselves and no one else. So, presumably, we wear slinky thongs and super-push-up bras not because they make us attractive to men, but because they make *us* feel good about *ourselves*. We spend hours at the mall snatching up the latest sexy trends because we are "comfortable" enough with our bodies to carelessly showcase them to the world. Our role-models are anorexic actresses who confidently declare that they are happy and fulfilled and not concerned about what anyone thinks of them.

We obey the tyranny of pop culture under the guise that we are free to do whatever we want, whatever makes *us* feel good. As modern young women, we have deluded ourselves into thinking we are empowered, but in reality we couldn't be more ensnared. We convince ourselves that we are making our own decisions, that we are listening to our own voice, but in truth we are like putty in the hands of the culture's warped agenda.

Young women today are supposed to be the most liberated, independent, confident, and fulfilled of any in history. But we are a desperate, lonely, insecure, and hopeless lot—plagued by eating disorders, abusive relationships, emotional breakdowns, and sexual chaos.

We've been looking for beauty in the wrong place. And our incessant search for beauty has stripped us of all that is truly beautiful.

Searching for Self-Worth

"You are special! You are unique! You have value!" Kevin Richards' face was full of sincerity and passion as he spoke the words. I was 14, and our entire youth group was gathered under a big oak tree on the front lawn of our church to hear Kevin's inspiring "devo" (his cool slang term for a devotional lesson). Today's lesson was on self-esteem.

"Now I know that the world is always trying to tell you that you aren't good enough," Kevin continued. "But in God's eyes, you are good enough! He wants you to feel good about yourself."

Beside me some husky football players shuffled awkwardly on the grass. A few girls behind me started whispering to each other. None of us really knew how to respond to Kevin's motivational talk. Everyone on the lawn that day was battling with intense insecurity, but it wasn't the kind of thing that you talked about or even acknowledged at the age of 14.

Kevin wasn't deterred by our lack of response. "I want all of you to go home today," he said earnestly, "and look in the mirror. And I want you to say to your reflection, 'I love you!' "

At that, most of the group broke into embarrassed laughter. Kevin held up his hands and smiled wryly. "Hey, guys, don't knock it 'til you try it!" Then his face grew serious again. "Listen, I know it is easy to laugh at a message like this. But this is serious to God. He wants you to learn how to love yourself."

Love yourself. It was a message that I heard often, in many different forms, throughout my young adult life. "It is important to feel good about who *you* are!"

If that were true, I reasoned, I was pursuing all the right things. Most of my time and energy was devoted to feeling good about *me*. That was why I pored over all those beauty and fashion magazines. That was why I spent so much time obsessing in front of the mirror. That was why I rushed out to the mall every weekend to buy the latest trends.

So why did I feel worse than ever about myself?

A conversation with my small-group leader—a pretty college freshman named Staci—brought yet another perspective. "God didn't design all women to look like the cover of *Vogue* magazine," she told our group of girls as we sat in a circle on the youth room floor. "He made you beautiful just the way you are."

Staci encouraged us not to obsess over our bodies or lament that we didn't look like *Sports Illustrated* swimsuit models. Rather, we were told we should learn to find and appreciate our own unique beauty and not buy into the world's standards.

"What about wearing makeup and cute clothes?" a 15-year-old named Veronica wanted to know. "Are we just supposed to ignore how we look?"

"Absolutely not," Staci replied confidently. "It is good to take care of your body; it's God's temple. Wear makeup. Wear the right clothes. Make the best of what He has given you. Just don't worry if you don't look like a Victoria's Secret billboard. Everyone has their own unique beauty. Accept yourself the way you are."

It seemed like a healthy perspective. Each week we girls would spend hours shopping for the right clothes, improving our skin and bodies, and envying TV stars as they flaunted their perfect figures. But on Sundays and Wednesday nights, we would be gallantly reminded, "You are beautiful the way you are!" This became an unofficial mantra that was chanted to girls in Christian circles, presumably to keep us from ending up with an eating disorder or plastic surgery fetish because we had bought into the world's impossible standards for beauty.

But in truth, it was about as effective as telling a dehydrated desert wanderer to declare "I am *not* thirsty!" just as his tongue dries up and sticks to the roof of his mouth. Eventually, his desperate desire for water becomes unbearable no matter how hard he tries to convince himself that he doesn't need it.

No matter how many times we told ourselves "I am beautiful the way I am!" we were still entrenched in a world that relentlessly declared otherwise. And our desperate need to be appealing to the world was still there, no matter how many times we tried to ignore it. Like a thirsty desert traveler imbibing water, we slurped up the culture's messages, even as we denied we were doing it.

The Guy Problem

Such is the dilemma of all too many Christian young women today. We are told to appreciate our own unique beauty and accept ourselves for who we are. Meanwhile, we are constantly assaulted by a world that insists we aren't alluring enough—that we need to change our bodies, our clothes, and our personalities in order to be more appealing. And it's not just the fashion industry and Hollywood that are to blame.

Guys are a huge part of the problem.

The same culture that trains us as young women to become sexy, sultry, and seductive also trains men to lust after women who possess those traits. "Guys think about sex every 3.5 seconds" is the message proclaimed by television, movies, and modern psychology. "Whenever a guy talks with a girl, he's not really thinking about the conversation. He's imagining what she looks like naked. It's just the way men are. Guys will be guys." This is what boys hear from the time they are old enough to even notice the opposite sex. They begin to believe that being lustful cavemen is the way they were created. It is implied that if a guy isn't consumed by sexual desires and erotic fantasies, he is completely abnormal.

Most of today's guys—even Christian ones—have bought into Hollywood's standards of beauty, drooling over sex queens and scorning all things pure, innocent, and uncorrupted. And living among them, we become convinced that we must scrape and claw to be noticed by guys, to cheapen ourselves to become desirable to anything male that moves.

We can tell ourselves that we appreciate our own unique beauty. We can say that we've learned to accept ourselves just the way we are. But the moment we walk out our front doors, we see clusters of guys drooling over any skimpily dressed, well-proportioned female who passes by. We watch them lustfully grin at sultry, bikini-clad models on the covers of magazines. We hear them talk about the incredible bodies of the hottest young singers or actresses on TV. We even catch many of them sneaking frequent peeks at Internet porn. And we start to question whether our own "special and unique qualities" will ever really be enough to turn a man's head, let alone win his heart.

Brittany, a spunky college sophomore, recently told me, "I want to be patient and wait for a Christlike guy. But I am afraid that if I don't throw myself at every guy who comes along, I'll never find someone. If I don't play the game, I'm afraid that no one will ever want me."

Brittany echoes the secret fears of countless thousands of girls in our generation. Telling ourselves we are "beautiful the way we are" doesn't convince us that a guy will one day appreciate our "unique" beauty. It doesn't quench our desperate longings to be found attractive and desirable.

Our lives reflect our inward desperation.

The world beckons us to become more appealing by imitating pop-culture trends and movie stars, while the church encourages us to love and accept ourselves the way we are. But neither message provides the true solution to our inner crisis.

We long to be found beautiful—to feel the gentle caress of an adoring man who is dazzled by our loveliness. But most of us have either given up on that dream altogether, or we have given up our innocence in the futile pursuit of it.

As women we were born with an intrinsic longing for our femininity to be appreciated. But in this world of unattainable standards for female perfection, is it possible to become a breathtakingly beautiful princess who will ravish the heart of a prince? Is it possible to not merely accept ourselves the way we are, but to actually become as spectacularly lovely, appealing, and valuable as our feminine hearts desire?

The answer is a resounding yes.

But just as lasting and fulfilling romance is not found in the place that most of us search for it, neither is feminine beauty found in the place that most of us seek it. There is only one path that leads to true beauty. It is a narrow, rocky, obscure road that is hidden from the eyes of most. There are only a few in every generation who find it. But those who do are the most blessed and radiant of all women.

Hollow Beauty

MARIA'S STORY A top fashion model—let's call her "Maria"—is considered by many to be a positive role model for Christian girls because she has taken a public stand against premarital sex (never mind all of her practically naked, sex-goddess poses that are lustfully viewed by millions of men). Maria has what most young women long for—worldly beauty, sex appeal, and the rapt attention of every guy she meets. She has the kind of life most of us would envy—men, money, fame, glamour, and luxury at her fingertips. She even has a relationship with God. Maria is a devout church-goer and is outspoken about premarital abstinence (which has earned her the title "the world's most voluptuous virgin" among the secular media).

But her first love is worldly applause. Her first and foremost pursuit is worldly beauty. She has gone to incredible lengths to fulfill the world's standard for feminine perfection. Everything about her perfect proportions and flawless skin has been artificially gained. "Everything about me is fake!" she admits. "From my hair to my nose to my toes." Then, as if suddenly struck by the emptiness of it all, she adds, "Even my heart is fake."[2]

Maria has the kind of life that most Christian girls are desperately seeking—a relationship with God combined with worldly applause, comfort, pleasure, and male attention. But for one who has supposedly reached the pinnacles of feminine beauty, the desires of her heart have not been met. Her relationship with God is only an afterthought to her first pursuit—worldly allure and approval. And even though the world applauds her beauty, she does not know true love, fulfillment, or joy.

Maria represents the path that the majority of modern Christian young women have chosen—a life built around the pursuit of worldly allure, beauty, and popularity and fitting a relationship with God in wherever it's convenient. But, as Maria's life demonstrates, even if we somehow attain the kind of worldly beauty we are seeking, we still will not find the kind of beauty that our hearts are desperately searching for.

Imagine having the kind of beauty that doesn't need to be "propped up" by artificial means, a beauty that doesn't merely last a few years and then fade with age, a beauty that will be cherished and appreciated for a lifetime.

If *that* kind of beauty could be found, even Maria would have to be intrigued.

The Secret Source of True Beauty

The world proclaims that female beauty is gained through diet pills, tanning booths, breast augmentation, and liposuction. Modern psychology and well-meaning Christian voices insist that beauty comes from within and that we merely need to love and accept ourselves the way we are.

If we pursue the world's version of beauty, we might end up with momentary applause, but like Maria, we will have only propped-up, fleeting beauty on the outside and a hollow, fake heart on the inside. If we take Kevin Richard's advice and learn to "love ourselves" and "embrace our own unique inner beauty," we find merely a cover-up, not a cure, for the deepest longings of our feminine hearts, like putting a Band-Aid over a staph infection and hoping it will go away.

Neither the world's version of beauty nor the modern self-esteem message truly fulfills our longing to shine with enchanting grace and princess-like dignity. And neither avenue meets that deeper inner desire to radiate with feminine beauty that never fades.

But there is another kind of womanly beauty—one that we don't hear much about in today's world. It's the dazzling loveliness of *set-apart femininity*.

Set-apart femininity exudes a beauty that is not of this world; it's the spectacular radiance of a woman completely transformed by the Author of all things lovely and pure.

Set-apart femininity, contrary to what you might be thinking, is not stodgy and grim-faced with drab, shapeless clothes, librarian glasses, and a 20-pound Bible under one arm. It's not hiding from society or shunning the opposite sex.

Set-apart femininity blends the classic womanly grace and dignity of an Audrey Hepburn with the sacrificial, poured-out-for-Christ lifestyle of an Amy Carmichael. It's true feminine beauty merged with absolute abandonment to Jesus Christ. It's the sparkling, vibrant, world-altering, Christlike version of femininity that your King created you to exude.

This kind of beauty is not found in the pages of fashion magazines. It's not found in the "love yourself" mantras of the modern self-esteem messages.

The spectacular sparkle of set-apart femininity is found through absolute abandonment to the Author of all true beauty. It's found by exchanging a life consumed with self for a life consumed with Jesus Christ, by trading the desire to be attractive to this world for the longing to be attractive to Him alone. Find a woman who cares about nothing but loving, serving, honoring, and glorifying Jesus Christ, and you will see who truly is "the fairest of them all."

Heavenly Beauty

JACKIE'S STORY Jackie Pullenger's life is the opposite of Maria's in just about every way. At 20 years old, she encountered Jesus Christ. He asked her to give up her family, comforts, and educational pursuits to lay down her life for some of the most destitute, dirty, and depraved people in the world—and she willingly obeyed. For more than 30 years she has lived among drug lords, heroine addicts, and prostitutes in an area that until recently was called the "Walled City of Hong Kong"—a sordid haven for appalling squalor, crime, and debauchery. While Maria spends her time trying the latest trends in makeup and clothes, Jackie stays up all night walking the streets and proclaiming the Gospel of Christ. While Maria is wined and dined by athletes and movie stars, Jackie shares her bowl of rice with hungry children. While Maria sleeps on silk sheets in luxury hotels, Jackie shares her cramped living quarters with 20 homeless people at once. Jackie even shares her bedroom with ex-prostitutes and drug addicts.

When I hear Maria speak, I am struck by her hollow, empty, unfulfilled life. When I hear Jackie speak, I am riveted by her stunning beauty, radiance, joy, and confidence. Maria supposedly has the life that all women want. But after a closer look, it's clear that Jackie, not Maria, has the life we all should envy.

Jackie is passionately in love with Christ. Because of her sacrificial devotion to Him, thousands of the most hopeless people in the world have been radically transformed, renewed, and set free. And when she speaks, it is obvious that she has something very few of us have ever tasted. "You may have your own bedroom," she says, "but I know God's grace."[3] While other women take delight in comfort, entertainment, romance, and pleasure, Jackie's treasures are found in an entirely different kingdom. Her life is straight after the pattern of the New Testament—"poor, yet making many rich; as having nothing, and yet possessing all things" (2 Corinthians 6:10). And as a result, she possesses the glorious radiance of a woman truly set apart for her King. Jackie does not have the applause of this world. But she has the applause of Jesus Christ, and to her that's all that matters.

Against all reason, against all odds, it is Jackie's life of poured-out devotion—not Maria's life of self-serving pleasure—that brings the fulfillment, contentment, and lasting beauty that we as women are desperately seeking.

A Whole New Pattern

Amy Carmichael (one of my heroes whose story I told in *Authentic Beauty*) once wrote about her frustrating search for set-apart women to join her in her ministry of rescuing Indian children from being sold into prostitution. "I wrote to all the pastors in the region, asking if they had any women wholly devoted to our Lord and separate in spirit from the world who were likely to be free for this work," she said. The pastors all replied the same, "Not only have we no women like this, but we do not know of even one woman of the kind you want."[4]

Sadly, what was true about young Christian femininity a hundred years ago is still true today. "Christian" young women are a dime a dozen in our country. But to find a young woman who is wholly devoted to Christ and separate in spirit from the world is rare indeed.

If we were given the choice between Maria's comfortable life of ease and worldly applause and Jackie's difficult life of sacrifice and worldly indifference, which would we choose? If we were to be honest, most of us would admit that it sounds far more appealing to "have our cake and eat it too," like Maria does. She goes to church, believes in saving sex until marriage, and claims to have a relationship with God. Yet she also has everything our selfish, sinful, pleasure-loving natures crave. It's a great combination; living a life of ease, comfort, and popularity, and still going to heaven in the end.

Jackie's life, to most of us, seems a little too extreme, a little too uncomfortable, a little too obscure. Why would we deliberately choose to give up all the pleasures and attractions of this world and live among the destitute and dying? Why can't we just serve God from the comfort of our air-conditioned homes?

It's a lot easier to build our lives around the pursuit of worldly applause and selfish pleasure and just fit Christ in somewhere on the side than to radically pour out our lives in sacrificial devotion to Him.

But the reason that we as modern young Christian women are so insecure, lonely, and unfulfilled is because we have chosen Maria's lifestyle instead of Jackie's. Maybe we aren't posing in racy underwear, but we are pursuing the very same shallow beauty, hollow approval of the world, and selfish pleasures, all the while proclaiming to be representatives of Christ.

Our lives do not reflect the stunning beauty of Jesus Christ; they reflect the shallow, imitation, pop-culture appeal of the world's system.

We live in a Christian world where Paris and Britney set the standard (or lack thereof) even for Christian girls, where oral sex is referred to by many as "Christian sex," and where Abercrombie catalogs, though labeled by many as "soft porn," strongly influence what Christian girls wear and how we wear it.

We live in a world where 200 Christian girls from a quiet church-going community had to be medically treated by the health department for an outbreak of syphilis because of their secret lives of sex and orgies—many of them admitting to having 50 or 100 different sex partners and engaging in sex acts with three guys at one time.[5]

We live in a world where radical abandonment to Christ means, at best, maintaining *technical* virginity until marriage and possibly going on a short-term mission trip every couple of years with iPod, cell phone, and *InStyle* magazine in tow.

A few months ago I listened as a group of "all-out-for-God" young women enthusiastically told me the name of their favorite movie. I knew which movie they were talking about. It included lengthy and graphic sex scenes, glorified rebellion against authority, and glamorized lust and betrayal—but it had "such a sweet ending!" and the girls had watched it many times. (Important side note: I looked up this movie on a parents' movie guide website that described all the questionable content in detail. Not only did the "sex/nudity" descriptions for this movie take up an entire page, they were far too graphic for me to even consider including in this book.)

Forgive me if I seem to be ranting, but I believe there is so much more to being a Christian young woman than what we have settled for today. Christian femininity has sunk to dismally low standards, and we are evidencing the consequences of our compromise in rocky romances, stressful family relationships, mediocre marriages, empty spirituality, and unhappy, unfulfilled lives.

I speak from personal experience when I say that our standards are dismally low. I was raised in church and accepted Christ into my heart as a child at vacation Bible school. Growing up, I knew that God had certain standards I was supposed to meet. And the last thing I wanted to do was to get on God's bad side. I took my Christianity seriously. I wanted to be pleasing to God. But I also wanted to be pleasing to the world. From the time I was 12 or 13, I began listening to lackadaisical Christian messages that justified my preoccupation with selfishness and pleasure. Fortunately for me, these were not hard to find.

"Five Ways to Have Fun with Your Friends" was the title of an article in a Christian magazine for young women that my parents had subscribed to on my behalf in the hopes that it would be a good influence on me. The article gave suggestions such as going to the mall and seeing who could buy the most creative thing for five dollars, staying up all night having a chick-flick marathon, and holding a lip-synching contest to your favorite pop songs. In other words, spending hours at the mall listening to countless messages of "here's how to be sexy" and "here's the latest thing that will make you cool!" was perfectly acceptable. Drinking in Hollywood's philosophy of romance and femininity was no big deal. And imitating a pop star's sultry rendition of a song about love-gone-wrong was just harmless fun.

"Which Hollywood celebrity would you rather be?" quizzed my Christian devotional for girls. "Julia Roberts, Catherine Zeta-Jones, or Sandra Bullock?" In other words, it was perfectly fine to look to sexy starlets as my role models for successful womanhood.

My youth group Bible study leader often challenged me and the other girls not to become discouraged if we didn't look like the girls on the cover of *Seventeen*. But she never challenged us not to read *Seventeen* in the first place.

Modern Christianity focused on helping me live at least somewhat morally in the midst of all the pop-culture attractions that constantly bombarded my senses. But it didn't challenge me to shift my affections away from pop-culture attractions altogether.

Like countless young women today, I lived with one foot in the world and the other in the murky waters of Christian compromise. I lived my life only two or three steps ahead of the culture's standards.

When it came to clothes—I dressed seductively, just not quite as slutty as the girls on the Guess jeans ads. When it came to role models—I revered popular young singers or movie stars who said they were Christians. (What did it matter if you really couldn't tell by their lives?) When it came to magazines—I read the style and beauty articles and (usually) skipped the ones that justified premarital sex. When it came to pastimes—I watched the same movies and listened to the same music as everyone else and tried to overlook all the profanity and perversion. When it came to guys—I flirted and cavorted like everyone else but made sure it was mostly with guys who claimed to be Christians and went to youth group. When it came to relationships—I gave myself emotionally and physically to one fling after another, but saved my "technical" virginity until marriage.

I was a "Christian" young woman. But I was not a set-apart young woman.

Still to this day, I am flooded with gratitude that God did not leave me in that state of mediocrity. Gently, patiently, and lovingly, He began to open my eyes to see how far from being His princess of purity I really was. And He began to show me a glorious new pattern for my life as a young woman—*His pattern*. It's a pattern that is continually being built and shaped within my life, even to this day. It's the pattern of set-apart femininity, and it's God's sacred intent for each of our lives.

This book doesn't present a comfortable message. It won't show you how to live a self-indulgent life with a little Christian morality tacked on. It won't give you tips on how to dress a tad less sexy than the Abercrombie billboards or how to get the attention of that hot Christian guy without coming across as desperate.

This book presents a vision for a whole different kind of Christian femininity than what we see all around us today. And if you allow it to, it will awaken you to a whole new way to live that will change your existence forever.

It *is* possible, even in today's world, to possess that spectacular, radiant, lasting feminine loveliness that we've dreamed about since childhood. And not only is it possible, it is God's sacred intent for each and every one of His daughters.

Joining the Ranks

What is the secret to great living? Entire separation to Christ and devotion to Him. Thus speaks every man and woman whose

life has made more than a passing flicker in the spiritual realm.
It is the life that has no time for trifling that counts.[6]

–Amy Carmichael

History is filled with amazing examples of stunning set-apart women, wholly devoted to Jesus Christ. Their awe-inspiring examples of radiant femininity put modern young women (myself included!) to shame. Here are some of my favorites.

Vibia Perpetua, one of the earliest Christian martyrs, was thrown into the arena among wild beasts and then killed with a gladiator's sword because of her faith in Christ. A beautiful young woman of high education and noble birth, she gladly gave up all worldly comforts and applause for the cause of Christ. The mother of an infant son whom she dearly loved, she could have obtained life and freedom simply by denying her faith in Christ. But, as it says in Revelation 12:11, she loved not her life unto death. Greatly rejoicing that she was counted worthy to suffer and die for her Savior, Vibia went to face the wild beast's attack singing a psalm with a joyful, radiant countenance. Walking confidently to her death, as Christ walked to Calvary, she was given victory over her senses and felt no pain, only a deep oneness with God. Just before she died, she exhorted her brother, who was watching, to stand fast in the faith. Like many other martyrs, her blood became the seed of the early Christian Church. Because of her courageous spirit and sublime faith, the Church drew in countless people who could not ignore the hope and heroism displayed in the life and death of this radiant daughter of the King.[7]

Elizabeth Fry, a young English wife and mother of 11 children in the late 1700s, became the sole instrument of prison reform for an entire continent as she followed the leading of her King Jesus. At the age of 17, she first encountered Jesus Christ, and from that moment on she never opened her eyes day or night without her first waking thought being how best she might serve her Lord. One day in 1813, she went to visit a women's prison in her town. When the doors closed behind her, she felt she had entered a den of wild beasts. The inhumane conditions, obscene language, foul odors, suffering, and depravity of the prisoners left her heart aching. From that moment on, she resolved to be Christ's hands and feet to the needy prisoners in her country.

Drawing supernatural strength from Christ, she restored dignity and humanity to thousands of filthy and depraved prisoners, she visited kings and magistrates, she petitioned courts, and she proposed new ordinances that completely transformed the prison system in Europe, all the while being an excellent and attentive mother to her large family. Because of her tireless life of sacrifice, thousands of prisoners were saved, both physically and spiritually. Hundreds embraced Christ because of her example. Even kings and government officials were forever altered by Elizabeth's life. An early American congressman who observed her work wrote this of her: "I have seen Elizabeth Fry and have witnessed her miraculous effects of true Christianity upon the most depraved of human beings. The wretched outcasts have been tamed and subdued by the Christian eloquence of Mrs. Fry. Nothing but God can effect such a miracle."[8]

Gladys Aylward was 25 when she met Christ and offered her life to Him fully and completely. He placed a heavy burden upon her heart for the suffering and unreached people of war-torn China. But she had no money, did not speak the language, and was unqualified to go alone to a dangerous and hostile land. Then one day she heard a challenge from her Lord, and she knew she had to go exactly where He was calling her—to China. At the age of 26, she boarded a train to China with only a small handful of coins in her pocket and embarked upon one of the most extraordinary adventures of all time.

Over the next 20 years, Gladys preached the Gospel to thousands of Chinese men and women, tended to hundreds of wounded soldiers during the war, single-handedly stopped a deadly riot at a men's prison, cared for the sick and lepers, and adopted more than a hundred orphans, often going without food so that they could survive. During the Japanese invasion, she was on the "dead or alive most wanted list" and at times narrowly escaped pursuers seeking to end her life—her clothing riddled with bullet holes.

She led 200 orphans on a six-week journey across the mountains to bring them to safety; a journey so exhausting that she lapsed into a coma as soon as the task was completed. Gladys's life of complete abandon to Jesus Christ literally changed the face of a nation. At the end of her life, she wrote: "My heart is full of praise that one so insignificant, uneducated, and ordinary in every way could be used to His glory for the blessing of His people in poor persecuted China." Though ordinary and insignificant, Gladys lived one of the most spectacular displays of triumphant femininity this world has ever seen, all because she staked everything upon the faithfulness of her God.[9]

Sabina Wurmbrand was the young wife of a pastor and mother of a little boy during the Communist takeover in Romania in 1949. At a pastor's convention, Sabina sat next to her husband as one Christian leader after the next walked onto the stage and blasphemed the name of Jesus Christ, caving to the demands of the Communist officials sitting in the front row. Her heart began to burn within her. She was passionately in love with Jesus Christ and could not stand to hear such things spoken about Him by His own people. She turned to her husband. "Will you not wipe the spit from the face of Christ?" she asked him. Richard pointed at the Communist officers. "If I stand up and speak against their agenda, they will kill me," he told her. Sabina did not hesitate. "I would rather be married to a dead man," she replied, "than to a coward." It was the infusion of strength Richard needed. He rose to his feet, sparked by the passion of his wife, and thunderously spoke truth in the midst of lies.

Sabina loved her husband and little boy. But she loved Jesus even more. She was willing to lay down every bit of personal joy, happiness, and security to see His name glorified. The next 12 years of Sabina's life were excruciatingly difficult because of the stand she had taken that day. Richard was imprisoned and tortured, and she had no way of knowing whether he was dead or alive. She was thrown into prison herself for four years, her little boy forced to fend for himself on the streets. When she was released, she was unable to buy or sell because of her status as the wife of a pastor and relied only on the kindness of others to survive. But to Sabina, it was more than worth it. No matter what hardships she faced, she never ceased to shine with joy, contentment, and Christlike beauty. She spoke of Jesus to anyone who would listen, even at risk of her own safety. Thousands discovered the transforming power of Christ through Sabina's incredible example of courage and devotion. To Sabina, every night of hunger, pain, and separation from her family was more than worth it. Jesus was everything to her. And her life was a glorious display of passionate devotion to Him at any cost.[10]

Answering the Sacred Call

The sacred call God placed upon these incredible women's lives is the very same call He has placed upon yours and mine. Only one question remains. Are we willing to lay down everything else and take up His set-apart commission?

God's sacred intent for us goes far beyond just saving sex until marriage, wearing one-piece swimsuits instead of skimpy string bikinis, or idolizing Christian bands instead of secular ones. It is not just making sure we tack on some Christian morality to our self-indulgent lives.

His sacred intent for you and for me is nothing short of absolute abandonment to Jesus Christ, entire separation from the pollution of the world, and ardent worship of our King with every breath we take.

Yes, it's a huge vision—one that is contrary to everything our culture presents. In our modern world, we as young women seem to be presented with only two options for our femininity—we can either embrace the sensual, sexed-up version of womanhood glorified by pop culture, or we can go the opposite direction and trade in perfume and makeup for grit, grunge, and guy-like behavior.

But both of these options cause us to completely miss out on the glorious pattern God designed for our femininity. We were created to shine with heavenly beauty, to radiate with Christlike feminine loveliness, and to sparkle with the lily-white purity of our Prince. We were created to be set apart for Him.

As you read this book, you will likely hear plenty of voices in the background screaming that it is impossible to achieve this set-apart standard. But the good news is—you don't have to achieve it on your own. As Oswald Chambers says,

> When we deliberately choose to obey God, He will tax the remotest star and the last grain of sand to assist us with all His almighty power.[11]

Whatever your version of femininity has been up to this moment—God desires to offer you hope and a glorious future. Jesus Christ can take a life that has been bruised, rejected, or squandered and make it completely new. He can empower a weak and helpless life to rise up and conquer. No matter where you've been or what you've done or how far from Him you feel right now—He can transform you into a radiant, victorious, world-changing, set-apart young woman.

No matter how worthless or ugly you feel, He longs to shape you into His stunning princess. It starts with one simple step of obedience—one simple decision to answer the sacred call He has upon your life…no matter what the cost.

Sacred Design
discovering femininity's blueprint for beauty

> You have ravished my heart, my sister, my spouse; you have ravished my heart with one look of your eyes (Song of Solomon 4:9 NKJV).

Jia was 16 when she answered the sacred call of the set-apart life. Growing up in a rural Chinese village, Jia struggled with her family to make ends meet. Life was harsh and her future seemed bleak. But then she met Jesus and everything changed.

Jia didn't merely say a prayer to accept Christ so that she could go to heaven someday. Rather, she came face to face with the King of all kings. She was awestruck by His incredible, everlasting love for her; a love that moved Him to give up His very life on her behalf. Jia responded to His amazing love by offering her entire existence to Him—a decision she knew would likely cost her everything.

Christianity is illegal in China. If Jia openly confessed her belief in Christ, there was a very good chance she would be thrown into prison and even tortured or killed. Her family would disown her, kick her out of the house, and leave her on the streets to fight for survival.

But what did all of that matter in light of all that Christ had done

31

for her? She was called to be a set-apart young woman for Jesus Christ, a living sacrifice for Him. She was willing to give her life for the One who had given everything for her. No price was too great to express her love and gratitude for Jesus Christ.

Jia told her parents she had accepted Christ. She was kicked out of the house immediately, sent away without so much as a second glance. From her parents' point of view, Jia no longer existed.

But Jesus was with her. He was all she needed.

Jia literally radiated with excitement about Jesus. Scrounging up a rickety bicycle and two cold potatoes, she set out with her friend Lin, who had also become a Christian and been disowned by her family.

Jia and Lin couldn't keep silent about the good news of Christ, though they knew that speaking about it would likely cost them their freedom. They began riding from village to village to proclaim the amazing message of the Gospel to everyone they met.

By the time they reached the first village, they had given away their potatoes, the only food they had, to a poor beggar in need. And by the time they reached the second village, they had given away the bicycle to someone else in need. This has been the pattern of Jia's life ever since.

Jia and Lin, to this day, continue traveling from town to town, sharing the love of Christ with everyone they encounter, sleeping on the ground, and literally trusting God for every meal.

Wherever they go, the girls' faces shine so brightly that people come up to them and stare. They radiate with an inner glow that cannot be manufactured or mustered-up. Their bodies are the temples of the King of all kings, and His Spirit cascades through them like a waterfall.

Jia has no Christian books to help prop up her faith. She has no youth group worship services to keep her on fire for God. She has no Christian summer camps to remind her that following Christ is cool; no Christian concerts to keep this whole Jesus thing fun.

All Jia has is an unshakable, passionate love for her Lord and King. This love has so completely transformed her life that everyone who meets her is envious of what she possesses—though she has absolutely nothing of material value or human comfort.

In my book *Authentic Beauty,* I shared my favorite quote from Elisabeth Elliot: "The preoccupations of young women don't seem to change much from generation to generation. But in every generation there seem to be a few who make other choices."[1]

Jia is one of the few. While scores of other Christian young women around the world are completely preoccupied with decisions about what to wear to the mall or which guy to go after, Jia is completely preoccupied with Jesus Christ. She is not living an easy life. But she is living the most exciting, radiant, world-changing, fulfilled life of any modern young woman I've ever seen.

What does Jia have that most modern Christian young women do not? A life fully and completely transformed by the power, life, and radiance of her heavenly Prince. Jia possesses more inward and outward beauty than any other young woman I've encountered. Why? Because her life is not her own. She has been bought with a price. And the life she now lives is *Christ in her* (see Galatians 2:20). Jia didn't just take the message of Christ as head knowledge—she actually allowed it to deliver her, heal her, restore her, capture her, empower her, and transform her.

The reason that modern Christian femininity falls so far short of Jia's breathtaking example of true beauty is because we do not understand the reality of who Jesus Christ is meant to be in our lives. Jesus is not meant to be slipped into our lives whenever it is convenient. He is not meant to be treated as a casual buddy we hang out with every once in a while. Jesus wants to be our life. He wants to occupy every waking thought, action, attitude, word, and decision.

What does it mean to be a Christian? As the late revivalist Leonard Ravenhill defined it: "Your life is hid with Christ. You are not your own. You have no time of your own, no money of your own. Christ must become your complete Master."[2]

If you are ready to trade the hollow self-made beauty of this world for the glorious Christ-built beauty of a set-apart young woman, this is where it all begins. Denying self, taking up your cross, and following the Lamb wherever He leads. In other words, letting go of all preoccupation with self: our comfort, our pleasure, our agenda, our popularity, our ability to gain the world's approval, even our own dreams and desires. And as Paul did, treating all those things as rubbish for the excellence of the knowledge of Him and the power of His resurrection and the fellowship of His sufferings (Philippians 3:7-9).

At first glance, it sounds like a scary decision to make. If we stop looking out for our own agendas and become completely preoccupied with Christ, won't our lives become dull, boring, and legalistic? If we forsake the Maria attitude and stop pursuing worldly applause, worldly beauty, and worldly pleasure, won't our lives lose all their luster?

Just the opposite. A life overtaken by the heavenly beauty of Christ is the only life truly worth living. Yes, it may include discomfort, prison, pain, or even death, but it also includes triumph, joy, peace, and fulfillment in their richest and purest forms.

I remember when God first challenged me to give up trying to write my own love story and allow Him to do with this area of my life exactly as He saw fit. I hesitatingly gave the "pen" of my love story to the Author of romance, worrying that I would end up with a bleak, drab, dismal, second-rate version of love as a result—or possibly end up as a lonely old woman, sitting in a rocking chair in a long, gray, shapeless dress and rocking my life away in misery. Now I laugh at my ridiculous fears. Jesus Christ takes very good care of the things we entrust to Him. The love story that He wrote for me was completely beyond anything I ever could have hoped for or imagined.

It's the same when we offer our existence to Him. We may not gain Maria's fame, fortune, or sex appeal, but we will gain all the riches of His kingdom. We will gain the lasting loveliness that every woman longs for. We will gain the unshakable fulfillment that the rest of this world spends their entire lives searching for in vain. Not only that, but we will gain real excitement and adventure. Instead of living vicariously through movie characters as they single-handedly save the world from nuclear disaster, we will actually live out the most spectacular real-life adventures this world has ever seen. Just think about the anything-but-dull lives of Vibia Perpetua, Elizabeth Fry, Gladys Aylward, and Sabina Wurmbrand!

> ...those who catch the vision are ready to follow the Lamb wherever He leads, and as they follow, in this spirit of joyful adventure, their path becomes clear before them and they are given power to fulfill their high calling. They are those who have the courage to break through conventionalities, who care not at all what the world thinks of them, because they are entirely taken up with the tremendous reality of Christ.[3]
>
> —Bishop Bardley

I don't know about you, but that sums up everything that I truly desire. Maria can keep her propped-up beauty, fleeting popularity, and fake heart. I want Jackie and Jia's version of radiance—the kind of beauty that never fades away. I want to join the ranks of set-apart femininity and glow with the kind of loveliness that all of heaven cheers.

Daily and continual surrender of every part of my life to Christ's lordship has not only been the best way to keep intimacy with Christ alive in my own life, but it is also my biggest and most difficult challenge! Because of our sinfulness as humans, surrender goes against every fiber of our utterly selfish beings, especially because we cannot physically "see" the One to whom we surrender. But, as Paul reminds us, "we walk by faith, not by sight." The key to the set-apart life is Christ's words, "If anyone desires to come after Me, let him deny himself, and take up his cross daily, and follow Me. For whoever desires to save his life will lose it, but whoever loses his life for My sake will save it" (Luke 9:23-24).

—Miriam, 24

Power to Fulfill the Call

When I was first married, I wasn't a huge fan of the larger-than-life example of womanhood portrayed in Proverbs 31. Getting up before dawn to "seek wool and flax and work eagerly with my hands" just didn't sound very appealing, and I felt confined by the image of the domestic diva whose life revolved around cooking, sewing, and caring for children.

Over the years, I've been around countless Christian women who shared those sentiments. "I'll become the Proverbs 31 woman just as soon as I get all those Proverbs 31 maids!" a young wife once jokingly told me.

"I'm so sick and tired of hearing about becoming a godly, Proverbs 31 woman!" a Christian college girl told me recently. "There is no way I would ever measure up to that standard, and I'm not even going to try."

It seems that in recent years, Christian femininity has decided to boycott heroic womanhood—especially when it comes in the form of the "stay-at-home supermom" portrayed in Proverbs 31.

In a world that is constantly telling us "you'll never be good enough," we squirm at a Biblical message that holds us to another seemingly impossible standard. We are tired of hearing about all the ways we don't measure up, and Proverbs 31 seems to only rub salt on a painful wound.

The authors of the popular Christian book *Captivating* (a book we will discuss in greater detail later in this chapter) express it this way: "We are all living in the shadow of that infamous icon, 'The Proverbs 31

Woman' whose life is so busy I wonder, when does she have time for friendships, for taking walks, or reading good books? Her light never goes out at night? When *does* she have sex? Somehow she has sanctified the shame most women live under, Biblical proof that yet again we don't measure up."[4]

Such sarcasm toward this particular section of the Word of God almost seems justified. After all, God doesn't want us to work ourselves to the bone trying to live out an impossible standard, does He? He doesn't want us to constantly feel guilty about how we are falling short, does He?

It's easy to just roll our eyes at Proverbs 31 and assume that there is some vague, allegorical reason why it was included in the Bible and that we certainly aren't supposed to apply its message to our daily lives. But a few years ago, I made some surprising discoveries about Proverbs 31 that shifted my perspective dramatically.

"Who can find a virtuous woman?" The word "virtuous" here is actually a masculine noun that means "strength, might, valor, and power." In other words, the Proverbs 31 woman is a mighty, valiant woman full of strength and conquering power. It's the very same word that is used to describe the valiance of David when the Lord chose him to be Israel's mighty king: "I have seen a son of Jesse the Bethlehemite, who is…a mighty man of valor, a man of war…and the LORD is with him" (1 Samuel 16:18-19).

David's mighty valor was unmatched. His power was superhuman. As a boy he killed lions and bears with his bare hands and single-handedly slew the greatest giant in the land. As a man, he valiantly led armies into battle and annihilated all the enemies of the Lord.

It's this very same heroic valor that marks the Proverbs 31 woman. She has superhuman strength. She has unmatched valor. She valiantly stomps out whatever stands in the way of God's purposes. Nothing hinders her. Her life is a living display of triumph, victory, and the glory of God. The chief word used to describe the Proverbs 31 woman is the word *strength*. It's mentioned no less than three times throughout the chapter, in addition to the "virtuous, valiant" opening description.

And by the way, the Proverbs 31 woman does a lot more than sew, cook, and teach kids. A closer study of her life reminds me of the set-apart women of history past; women like Gladys Aylward, Amy Carmichael, and Elizabeth Fry—women who sacrificially poured out their lives for the poor, who rescued the oppressed from their enemies, who set captives free, and who transformed entire countries by their valiant, living testimony of God's power.

Contrary to what *Captivating* and many other modern Christian voices imply, the Proverbs 31 woman is not harried and haggard, never having time to slow down and take care of herself. It says that "she makes coverings for herself; her clothing is fine linen and purple... Strength and dignity are her clothing, and she smiles at the future" (Proverbs 31:22,25 NASB). That doesn't sound to me like a stressed-out, overtired, overworked, exhausted woman. In fact, it sounds a lot like my definition of set-apart femininity—the grace and dignity of an Audrey Hepburn blended with the poured-out devotion of an Amy Carmichael.

The long and short of it is that the Proverbs 31 woman is a set-apart woman. She lives a miraculous, superhuman, victorious, amazing, fulfilling, poured-out life. She is stunningly beautiful, dignified, and strong; stronger than every other woman around her. But here is the key—the source of her strength does not lie within herself. She relies on a power wholly not her own. Just like David, her superhuman strength comes from God alone. David expressed it this way:

> "You are my lamp, O LORD. The LORD shall enlighten my darkness. For by You I can run against a troop; by my God I can leap over a wall. As for God, His way is perfect. The word of the LORD is proven. He is a shield to all who trust in Him. For who is God, except the LORD? And who is a rock, except our God? God is my strength and power, and He makes my way

perfect. He makes my feet like the feet of deer, and sets me on my high places. He teaches my hands to make war so that my arms can bend a bow of bronze. You have also given me the shield of Your salvation. Your gentleness has made me great" (2 Samuel 22:29-36).

Because of the power of God, David was able to accomplish things that a mere human never could. It's the same with the set-apart life. We are called to live superhuman lives—to live an existence that other women would never attempt.

And we are not called to do this in our own strength—because it is impossible. The power to fulfill the high calling upon our lives was purchased by the blood of our heroic King.

Who can find a virtuous woman? For her price is far above rubies. (Proverbs 31:10 KJV).

Jesus paid the ultimate price for His bride—He bought us with His blood, so much more precious than rubies. And this purchase was not just for the forgiveness of our sins, but to enable us to live valiant, superhuman lives that we could never live on our own—lives that truly showcase His stunning beauty, strength, and glory.

Instead of just rolling our eyes at the high call of the set-apart life, it's time we recognize and embrace the supernatural power that *Christ* provides to equip us to live triumphant, victorious, valiant lives—lives that literally shock this world around us.

Strength to Overcome

The birth of my son, Hudson, two years ago was the most intense and excruciating experience of my life thus far. Eric and I had chosen to have a home birth, with no drugs, painkillers, or option for surgery, a decision that I began to acutely regret about halfway into the process! The average labor is 10 to 12 hours. Mine was 39 hours long. And I felt every minute of it.

Hour after agonizing hour, I lay in misery on the bathroom floor, too weak to do anything but groan. I was too nauseated to eat or even drink much. My only nourishment came from the tiny spoonfuls of yogurt or juice that Eric or our midwife would shove into my mouth every 20 minutes or so. Agonizing pain seared through my stomach and lower back, shocking my entire body with its relentless intensity. The contractions were mercilessly sharp and frequent, coming every two or three minutes. But to my utter discouragement, the midwives told me I was not even close to the point of delivery. On and on the nightmare went, hour after hour, until I literally felt that I would die. I hadn't slept or eaten in nearly two days, and my body was racked with the most severe pain I'd ever thought possible. I couldn't speak. I couldn't move. I could only lie there in utter anguish, moaning and sobbing in sheer misery. How much longer could this continue?

After about 29 hours of this, I hit a wall of total despair. I could feel my body collapsing under the exhaustion and pain. I had reached the end of my own willpower. I had reached the end of my own strength. I had long since reached the end of my own determination. I knew I couldn't go on.

It was at that moment that I knew I had to make a choice. If I listened to my own body and mind, I would panic, despair, and crumble under the weight of this suffering. I was desperate to control the situation—to fight for my own comfort and alleviate my misery. But there was another voice within me, and He was gently asking for control. I was afraid to surrender the situation to Him. I was afraid that He would keep me in this anguish, that He would take me through more of this hell, that He would require more of me than I could give. And yet, His gentle whisper nudged me forward.

Lord, this body is not my own, it is Yours, I prayed inwardly. *I surrender to You. Whether You allow this agony to continue for one minute or another 20 hours, I yield to You. Take this body and do with it what You will. Showcase Your miraculous power in and through me now.*

As soon as I prayed the words, I felt an amazing, supernatural power course through me. Against all reason, I had hope. Against all odds, I had strength. No longer was I trying to bear the pain and suffering alone—He was bearing it for me. No longer was I fighting to end the agony—I was embracing it as a gift from Him. The sheer intensity of the situation had forced me to lean on the arm of my Bridegroom. It had chased me into His arms.

The pain did not lesson—it only grew more excruciating. The exhaustion did not disappear—it only grew more severe. The labor did not end—it lasted another ten hours, through the longest night of my life. And yet, He was carrying me. He was showcasing His strength through my being as hour after hour wore on.

As the light of the morning sun began to gleam through the bedroom windows, Eric grabbed a Bible from the bedside table and began to read the first Scripture his finger happened to fall upon: "Unto us a Child is born, unto us a Son is given (Isaiah 9:6)." My water broke just as he read the words, and Hudson's delivery finally began.

When Hudson was born, after my 39-hour ordeal, it was not the beautiful moment I had always imagined. I was too weak to even lift my arms to hold my baby. My body shook uncontrollably from sheer exhaustion, and sharp contractions continued for hours, even after the birth. I was in a fog of near unconsciousness. But I had never been more aware of His presence overtaking my being, His strength coursing through me. And I knew that He had given me something that could never be taken away—a glimpse of what is possible when I yield my body, my life, and my control to Him.

Three days after Hudson's birth, I received yet another opportunity to yield my body to my Lord and allow Him to do the impossible through me. I had developed a severe breast infection, which caused Hudson not to get any milk when he tried to nurse. We didn't realize the problem until it was almost too late. He was rushed to the hospital and diagnosed with starvation and dehydration. He was listless and lethargic and not even able to take fluids from a bottle. They hooked him up to IVs, a catheter, and a heart monitor and placed him in a glass incubator. Once again I was unable to hold my baby. Eric was requested to leave the hospital because he was incredibly sick with the flu and the doctors didn't want him to expose Hudson or me to the virus. I was left alone to face the crisis. I had not slept in nearly five days. I was barely able to stand because my body was still so weak from the 39-hour labor. I was shaking with fever and infection. And I was afraid for my baby's life.

When the doctor came into the room and rattled off a long list of all the serious problems Hudson might have, I could feel my emotions spiraling out of control. The nurse came in to take a blood sample. She brushed rudely past me and carelessly poked Hudson's tiny arm with a needle until she finally found a vein. It was all I could do to keep from screaming at her.

After the doctor and nurse were gone, I stood alone in the room, watching my helpless baby through a glass case. He had tubes covering nearly every part of his body, and his heart monitor beeped intermittently. It was another moment of choice. My body, mind, and emotions wanted desperately to collapse, to despair, to panic, and to scream in anger and hopelessness. But His Life within me wanted to showcase supernatural strength and hope. And once again, I prayed the words, *I surrender, Lord. My life is not my own, it is Yours. Showcase Your supernatural strength in and through me.* And once again, I tapped into a power that was not my own.

When my mom arrived at the hospital an hour later, she expected to find me hysterical. Instead, I was calm and peaceful—beyond all human reason. His power was in me, enabling me to do what was not possible on my own.

God's power and faithfulness were demonstrated right before my eyes. Hudson made a dramatic recovery, and within 24 hours after this ordeal, he was eating, growing, and thriving.

How have set-apart women throughout history faced incredible odds and triumphed? How did a 20-year-old girl named Jackie live among the most filthy, detestable people in the world and count it the greatest privilege of her life? How did an uneducated parlor maid named Gladys single-handedly stop a bloody prison riot and lead 200 orphans over the mountains to safety? How did a 19-year-old girl named Vibia face a violent public death while singing a joyful song of praise to her King?

Because their lives were not their own. Their bodies were not their own. They had become the dwelling place of Jesus Christ. He was their complete Master. They did not look at the set-apart life as a burden. They did not see the heroic call of Proverbs 31 as something they were meant to accomplish on their own. They understood how to yield to *His* power. They understood what Paul meant when he said, "I have been crucified with Christ; it is no longer I who live, but Christ lives in me" (Galatians 2:20).

Hudson's birth demonstrated to me, with incredible clarity, what is possible when I yield fully to His life within me rather than relying on my own agenda, my own control, and my own determination.

Now it is my desire and goal to yield to His stunning supernatural power not just in dire circumstances, but every moment of every day. Allowing His transforming life to overtake us is the secret to living the set-apart life in all its fullness, glory, and triumph.

The Modern "Inner Beauty" Myth

Why do we stop short of the incredible vision of radiant, set-apart femininity He desires to showcase in and through our lives? Because we don't truly grasp our utter helplessness; our absolute desperate need for all that He is. We don't understand that apart from Him, we *have* nothing, we *are* nothing, and we can *accomplish* nothing. We are still looking within ourselves to find beauty and strength that can come only from Him.

For me, like many other girls, the seeds for this struggle were planted at an early age. At my sixth-grade graduation, I stood with my fellow classmates on the creaky wooden risers in the school gym and belted out the popular Whitney Houston song "The Greatest

Love of All." As moms dabbed at their eyes, dads fiddled with video cameras, and Ms. Peterson (the plump and passionate choir teacher) frantically waved her arms in the vain hope of keeping us on rhythm, our squawky adolescent voices filled the air, heroically proclaiming that we had discovered all the beauty we possessed inside and learned to love ourselves, which apparently was the greatest love of all.

Even at the age of 12, I caught the irony of the moment. Here we were, a bunch of desperately insecure, awkward, gangly preteens, none of whom felt even the remotest sense of self-confidence, proudly declaring that we had learned to love ourselves. I assumed that our teachers and school counselors had conspired together to make us sing this ridiculous song, thinking that somehow just uttering those illustrious words might magically raise our self-esteem level.

It didn't work—at least not for me. I still felt like an ugly, self-conscious, out-of-style, out-of-touch little kid just trying to get through each day without ridicule from my peers. But everywhere I went, from school to church to teen magazines, I heard about this elusive "inner beauty" that I supposedly possessed. From rousing speeches by school counselors and Kevin Richards' repeated "devos" on self-esteem, I got the impression that if I could only learn how to tap into my own unique beauty and learn to love myself, all my insecurity problems would be solved, and I would no longer care what anyone thought of me. But for some reason, I never could find my own unique and special beauty.

And now I know why...because it didn't exist. Yes, that sounds a bit harsh, I know. But it's the truth.

Despite the well-meaning Christian campaign to boost the modern young woman's self-confidence, the reality is that we *do not possess anything beautiful or worthwhile in and of ourselves.* If we obtain a worldly outer beauty, Maria-style, we only have a propped-up, hollow, fleeting appeal that quickly fades with time and age. As Proverbs 31:30 says, "Charm is deceitful and beauty is passing." And if we muster all the human heroism and try to become a "good person," we only have a self-made, faltering form of goodness that can never stand against the stunning righteousness of Jesus Christ. Isaiah 64:6 says it perfectly: "We are all like an unclean thing, and all our righteousnesses are like filthy rags; we all fade as a leaf, and our iniquities, like the wind, have taken us away."

At first glance, it may appear to be a wonderful and even spiritual-sounding message to discover our own beauty and learn to love and accept ourselves "just the way we are." But if we rely on something that *we* possess to make us beautiful, we cannot receive the supernatural, transforming beauty of Jesus Christ.

This is the whole point of the Gospel; the whole message of what Christ does for us. We must lay down *everything* of self and be overtaken by a power, strength, beauty, and grace that is wholly not our own. That's when we find the ability to live out the supernatural, divinely beautiful, valiantly heroic Proverbs 31 life that He has called us to live as set-apart women.

> We are to be perfect as our Father in heaven is perfect, not by struggle and effort, but by the impartation of that which is Perfect.[6]
>
> —OSWALD CHAMBERS

The popular modern message for Christian women, found in books like *Captivating* and in exhortations given at women's church retreats, seeks to set us free to fully be ourselves, not hampered by insecurities caused by cultural messages and emotional wounds from the past. They rightly diagnose our intrinsic feminine desires to be found beautiful and rightly remind us that God wants to set us free to become the radiant childhood princesses of our dreams. But the solution presented, all too often, does not flow from the true Gospel of Jesus Christ. Why? Because it keeps *self* alive. It convinces us that we can look inward and find worth, beauty, and value within ourselves. It keeps the focus on *us;* on *our* feelings, *our* attributes, and *our* beauty. Here is how the authors of *Captivating* put it: "The beauty of a woman is first a soulful beauty. And yes, as we live it out, inhabit our beauty, we do become more lovely. More alluring. As the poet Gerard Manley Hopkins wrote, 'self flashes off frame and face.'…We want you to hear clearly that beauty is an essence every woman carries from the moment of her creation. The only things standing in the way of our beauty are our doubts and fears and the hiding and striving we fall to as a result."[6]

It sounds so right. But the Bible makes it very clear that we were born into sin, not beauty. Yes, we were created in the image of God. But sin has warped and twisted all the goodness and loveliness we were originally designed to possess. As a result of sin's defilement, we no longer carry an essence of beauty from the moment of our creation—we carry an essence of sin and selfishness. Our womanly souls are no longer beautiful. They are revolting, ugly, and deformed. That's why we need to be completely and wholly redeemed and remade by the power of Christ's blood.

Our sinful, self-loving nature urges us to buy into the idea that in and of ourselves we are important, noticed, and captivating. Yet the truth of the Gospel is not based on our intrinsic loveliness, but the fact that Christ loved us even *while we were yet sinners,* naked and covered in our own blood and shame (see Ezekiel 16:6).

Do we have value to God even before we are redeemed? Yes! God does love us and see us as valuable before we are redeemed, but it's *not* because we are attractive to Him and it's not because we possess anything worthwhile—inwardly or outwardly. It is because He Himself is Love personified, and He longs to rescue us from our ugly, reviled state and place *His* divine, heavenly beauty upon us. The great preacher Charles Spurgeon said it perfectly: "If a soul has any beauty, it is because Christ has endowed that soul with His own, for in ourselves we are deformed and defiled! There is no beauty in any of us but what our Lord has worked in us."

Any human beauty, any human value that we might find within ourselves is just a filthy rag compared to the limitless beauty and glory of Jesus Christ. Christ's beauty is perfect. And, in spite of what we deserve, He desires to adorn us with His spectacular glory. He may choose to showcase His beauty through us in a unique way, through our own individual personalities or the special gifts He has given us. But it is not *our* unique beauty that must shine for this world to see. It is not *our* own beauty that we must discover and embrace—*it is His.*

World-altering, set-apart, Christ-shaped femininity throughout history has never been concerned with thoughts of "inhabiting our own beauty" or letting "self flash off frame and face." Rather, a set-apart woman is consumed with the desire to have *Christ* flash off her frame and face and letting *Christ* (not self) inhabit every part of her inner being.

Vibia Perpetua, Elizabeth Fry, Gladys Aylward, Sabina Wurmbrand, and Amy Carmichael all had very different stories and very different ways in which Christ's beauty was showcased through their lives. But their lives all echoed the same heart's cry, "I must decrease, so that He might increase!" (see John 3:30).

We will not overcome our insecurities and gain the sparkling confidence we long for by singing "The Greatest Love of All" or reading books that exhort us to "live out our own beauty." And we will not become world-changing, set-apart women by letting "self flash off frame and face." The secret to becoming the radiant, beautiful, alluring, lily-white princess of childhood dreams is *forgetting all about self* and becoming completely consumed with only one thing—*Jesus Christ.*

> The Christian life can be explained only in terms of Jesus Christ, and if your life as a Christian can still be explained in terms of you—your personality, your willpower, your gift, your talent, your money, your courage, your scholarship, your dedication, your sacrifice, or your anything—then although you may have the Christian life, you are not yet living it.[7]
>
> —Ian Thomas

Christ said, "Whoever desires to come after Me, let him deny him-self, and take up his cross, and follow Me" (Mark 8:34 NKJV). The word "deny" here literally translates: to forget one's self, lose sight of one's self and one's own interests. We are meant to let all thoughts of self become swallowed up in Him.

> It is a tremendous freedom to get rid of all self-consideration and learn to care about only one thing—the relationship between Christ and ourselves.[8]
>
> —Oswald Chambers

In the heart of every young woman lies the intrinsic desire to be found beautiful. But when we come to Jesus, we exchange our desires to be noticed and appreciated for the desire that He and He alone would shine gloriously through our beings. Maybe no one will ever notice us. But that makes no difference as long as they notice *Him* shining through us. We can waste precious time and energy searching for something of worth and value in our own souls. Or we can join the ranks of historical set-apart women and declare, "less of me and more of Him!" That is when our souls will sparkle with the spectacular beauty of Jesus Christ.

The modern self-worth message says that a woman who is fully alive to herself is a woman who is truly beautiful. But the Biblical and historical message of set-apartness proves that a woman who is completely *dead* to herself and alive to Christ (like Jia, Jackie, Vibia Perpetua, Elizabeth Fry, Gladys Aylward, and Sabina Wurmbrand) is truly the fairest of them all.

Personally, I never saw stunning feminine beauty until I encoun-tered women who were completely unaware of self and completely consumed with their precious King. And now I know what kind of beauty I want to seek with all my heart. Not a beauty that can be found within my own soul, but a beauty that is entirely other-worldly in nature, a beauty that flows from the only One who is truly beautiful.

"Your fame went out among the nations because of your beauty, for it was perfect through My splendor which I had bestowed on you," says the Lord GOD. "But you trusted in your own beauty...such things should not happen, nor be" (Ezekiel 16:14-16 NKJV).

Making It Practical

The First Step: Embracing Our Unworthiness

Shannon is a young college student in a serious fog of guilt and shame. "I have messed up my life so much that I wonder if God can really forgive me or love me," she wrote in an email to me. "I walk around all the time feeling guilty and hating myself. I think I've gone too far for Him to make anything good out of my life."

Many of us can relate to Shannon's struggle. We wonder how to truly receive the forgiveness of Christ. The enemy of our souls whispers viciously in our ears, telling us that we are unworthy, that our pasts are too marred, that our souls are too dirty to ever be washed clean and marked by His divine beauty. It sounds harsh to tell Shannon that she possesses nothing of real beauty or value and that she is utterly unworthy to receive the transforming love of Christ.

But that's the exact message that Shannon—and all of us—must first understand to be remade by the stunning beauty of Christ. We *are* unworthy. Our souls *are* dirty. True repentance starts by acknowledging those facts. We are defiled and tainted. We are utterly unfit to bear His holy name. But it's not about our worthiness. *It's about His.*

Shannon does not need a "devo" from Kevin Richards about how to love herself. She does not need to be told that she has a beauty all her own and that she only needs to "inhabit that beauty." Rather, Shannon's deliverance and freedom will come when she *embraces* her own unworthiness and acknowledges that she has no hope outside of the redeeming power of Jesus Christ.

This is true repentance. Yes, it is hard to admit how far we have fallen. It is relentlessly hard on our selfishness and pride to face the fact that we are deformed and defiled. But it is only when we know how great our debts are that we can understand the gravity and wonder of what Jesus Christ has done for us. Only then can we love Him with unreserved devotion and gratitude. Just look at this powerful story about a woman who had much to be forgiven.

> And behold, a woman in the city who was a sinner, when she knew that Jesus sat at the table in the Pharisee's house, brought an alabaster flask of fragrant oil, and stood at His feet behind Him weeping; and she began to wash His feet with her tears, and wiped them with the hair of her head; and she kissed His feet and anointed them with the fragrant oil.
>
> Now when the Pharisee who had invited Him saw this, he spoke to himself, saying, "This Man, if He were a prophet, would know who and what manner of woman this is who is touching Him, for she is a sinner."
>
> And Jesus answered and said to him, "Simon, I have something to say to you."
>
> So he said, "Teacher, say it."
>
> "There was a certain creditor who had two debtors. One owed five hundred denarii, and the other fifty. And when they had nothing with which to repay, he freely forgave them both. Tell Me, therefore, which of them will love him more?"
>
> Simon answered and said, "I suppose the one whom he forgave more."
>
> And He said to him, "You have rightly judged." Then He turned to the woman and said to Simon, "Do you see this woman? I entered your house; you gave Me no water for My feet, but she has washed My feet with her tears and wiped them with

the hair of her head. You gave Me no kiss, but this woman has not ceased to kiss My feet since the time I came in. You did not anoint My head with oil, but this woman has anointed My feet with fragrant oil. Therefore I say to you, her sins, which are many, are forgiven, for she loved much. But to whom little is forgiven, the same loves little."

Then He said to her, "Your sins are forgiven...your faith has saved you. Go in peace" (Luke 7:37-50).

Simon the Pharisee didn't feel he really needed a Savior. He treated Christ as a casual buddy, hoping perhaps to glean some interesting insight or personal benefit from being around Him. But the sinful woman knew that Jesus Christ was her only hope. She had come face to face with the ugliness and horror of her defilement. She had accepted her utter unworthiness. And because of this, she could truly receive the mercy and forgiveness of her Lord. She threw herself at His feet in unreserved devotion and gratitude. That is true repentance.

Often we think of coming to Christ as a decision to "accept Him," to mentally acknowledge that He died, rose again, ascended into heaven and will return someday to take us to heaven. But repentance isn't merely the choice to "accept" Him and acknowledge those facts. Rather, it's falling at the feet of Jesus just like the sinful woman, fully aware that He is our only hope. It's crying out to Him from the depths of our soul, "Lord, have mercy on me, a sinner!" (see Luke 18:13).

When we have been forgiven much, we love Him much. Don't shy away from your feelings of unworthiness and hide behind flowery messages about embracing your own inherent beauty. *Acknowledge* the ugliness of your condition, the awfulness of your sin. Then embrace the awesome sacrifice He made on your behalf. To doubt His ability to forgive you is to question whether His sacrifice was really enough, whether He truly paid the penalty for your sin once and for all.

We only need to read the Gospels to be assured that He *did* pay the price for our sins—once and for all. Let us not cheapen His amazing sacrifice by questioning whether His work on the cross was truly enough. We are either ignorant or arrogant if we believe that Christ's death was not enough to cover *our* sins. At the moment Christ gave up His life for us, He proclaimed, "It is accomplished" (see John 19:30). The price had been paid. The power of sin had been conquered. It was done. It was final. It was absolute. He left no room for us to question it.

Don't try to add to His sacrifice by improving yourself before you fall at His feet in repentance. Simply come to Him, in all of your sin and weakness. Let Him wash you clean and make you completely new. Don't focus on your unworthiness. Rather, fix your eyes on the awesome power of His conquering, redeeming, transforming blood, shed on your behalf.

If you feel uncertain how to begin this process, I would encourage you to set aside a long period of time to be alone with Christ. Go somewhere you won't be distracted or interrupted. I often like to find a quiet place outdoors and have worship songs or audio Scripture playing on my iPod and my journal and Bible in hand. Come to Christ just as you are, asking Him to forgive you, renew you, wash you clean, and begin to shape you into His beautiful, set-apart princess. (If there are any ungodly habits, sinful addictions, or emotional baggage in your life that are hindering real intimacy with Christ, I would encourage you to work through the "Cleaning Out the Sanctuary" process found at www.setapartgirl.com. This material is very detailed and can be a great catalyst for removing all that stands in the way of our moving forward with Him.)

The Next Step: Being Made New

In *Authentic Beauty*, I wrote about encountering Jesus Christ as so much more than just my Savior—He became the Prince of my heart, the Lover of my soul, and the Lord of my existence. Instead of finding fulfillment through chasing after short-term flings with guys, I learned to find the deepest desires of my heart met in a romance with my heavenly Prince. Instead of desperately seeking to become attractive to the opposite sex, I now desired to be beautiful in *His* eyes.

But trying to become beautiful to Him on my own was like trying to create a sparkling, priceless jewel out of a worthless, dirty pebble. It couldn't be done. And yet, He was ready to make me completely new so that I could shine with a radiance that could never be taken away.

Most of us don't ever fully receive the transforming power of Christ because we don't fully understand the message of the Gospel. Take a few moments to join me in my own journey through Ezekiel 16:4-13, where God is speaking both to the nation of Israel and to each of us as individuals. As you do, allow God to speak to you specifically about the redeeming, transforming, beautifying work He desires to accomplish in *your* life.

> On the day you were born your navel cord was not cut, nor were you washed in water to cleanse you. You were not rubbed with salt nor wrapped in swaddling cloths. No eye pitied you, to do any of these things for you, to have compassion on you, but you were thrown out into the open field, when you yourself were loathed on the day you were born.

I was born into sin and ugliness. Because of sin's rule over me, I was deformed, defiled, and despised—thrown out into an open field like garbage, covered in my own filth and blood...the blood of my guilt and shame. There was nothing worthy or noble within me. I deserved nothing but death.

And yet, against all reason, that is not where my story ended, for Ezekiel 16 continues:

> "When I passed by you and saw you struggling in your own blood, I said to you 'Live!' I spread My wing over you and covered your nakedness. Yes, I swore an oath to you and entered into a covenant with you, and you became Mine," says the Lord GOD.

The God of the universe, the Author of all that is good and lovely, passed by and saw me in my wretched, hopeless condition. He was not attracted to my beauty or goodness because I had none. I had absolutely nothing to offer him. I was ugly and helpless, drowning in the blood of my own guilt and condemnation.

But incredibly, beyond all logic, beyond all comprehension, He had compassion on me. He rescued me. He entered into a covenant with me. He made me His own.

And for the first time, I had hope. I had a future. I had worth. Not because I possessed those things within myself—but *because I now belonged to Him.*

I was His child. But even that wasn't the end of the story.

> Your breasts were formed, your hair grew, but you were naked and bare.

He had rescued and redeemed me—but I was still naked and bare, utterly unable to showcase any true beauty on my own. I had tried to fulfill my desire for feminine beauty outside of Him. I had spent years trying to make myself more appealing, more valuable, and more desirable to everyone else but Him. And I had only succeeded in achieving a hollow, lifeless beauty that might temporarily appeal to the world but did not move the heart of my true Prince. No matter how I adorned myself with feminine allure on the outside, I was naked and bare of real beauty on the inside. I had not achieved even a speck of lasting loveliness.

He gently whispered to my soul that He wanted to place *His* perfect beauty upon me. He desired to transform me into a breathtaking princess who would ravish and captivate His heart. He wanted to adorn me with His glory, to dress me in royal garments, and to endow me with His splendor. But for that miracle to happen, I must first surrender to His cleansing, refining work.

> "Then I washed you in water. Yes, I thoroughly washed off your blood, and I anointed you with oil. I clothed you in embroidered

cloth and gave you sandals of badger skin. I clothed you with fine linen and covered you with silk. I adorned you with ornaments, put bracelets on your wrists, and a chain on your neck. And I put a jewel in your nose, earrings in your ears, and a beautiful crown on your head. Thus you were adorned with gold and silver, and your clothing was of fine linen, silk, and embroidered cloth. You ate pastry of fine flour, honey, and oil. You were exceedingly beautiful, and succeeded to royalty. Your fame went out among the nations because of your beauty, for it was perfect through My splendor which I had bestowed on you," says the Lord GOD.

As this Scripture expresses, I did not automatically radiate with His royal beauty simply because He had rescued me from sin and death. In order for His spectacular beauty to come cascading through my being, there was a major transformation process—a spiritual makeover—that was required.

I had to allow Him to thoroughly wash me clean, to remove the residue of sin and selfishness at the core of my life. I had to allow Him to remove the worldly garments that had cloaked my existence—my entrenchment in worldly attractions and interests— and clothe me in His royal garments of holiness. I had to allow Him to place His jewels on my body and His beautiful crown upon my head, marking me as consecrated and set apart for Himself like a lily among thorns.

And when I became set apart for Him, when I laid down my own selfish pursuits and allowed Him to completely transform my existence with His own breathtaking beauty—that's when all my girlish dreams were fulfilled. That's when I became the radiant princess I'd always longed to be—one who captivated the heart of my Prince with one glance of my eyes.

I discovered the secret of true feminine beauty when I embraced a beauty that was wholly not my own.

Even now the transforming process continues. There is always more selfishness to be cleansed and removed so that more of His glorious essence can radiate unhindered through my existence. There is always more of my life that must be refined and shaped by His royal beauty.

But I no longer pursue the empty, temporary beauty of this world. I no longer seek to be alluring to society. I seek to be beautiful to Him. I desire any outward beauty I possess to only be a reflection of my inner life—a life that has been fully captured and renovated by the noble Prince of my soul.

Take some time to ask yourself a few tough questions...and answer as honestly as possible. Does your life reflect the stunning beauty of Christ, or merely a hollow beauty or goodness of your own making? Are you a set-apart young woman, wholly and completely caught up in Him, or are you a self-focused young woman, wholly and completely caught up in your own whims and desires?

No matter where you have been or where you are at, Christ is ready to transform you with His stunning beauty. It won't be an instant, overnight transformation. But there is no better time to take the first step. Steal away alone with Christ and lay your life before Him. Allow Him to gently reveal to you the selfish patterns of your life and ask Him to forgive you and remake you in each of those areas.

Throughout the rest of this book, we will explore the practical, day-to-day life of a set-apart young woman. But this is where it all begins. Acknowledging that we have nothing. Receiving His transforming work. Being implanted with His divine, enabling grace to live lives we could never live on our own.

You may feel far away from such a life right now. But all that He asks is that you lay your life before Him so that He might begin His supernatural, incredible, life-altering work within you. If you come to Him holding nothing back, you will be amazed at how quickly He draws near to you (see James 4:8).

Have you ever wondered what it really means to "follow" Jesus Christ? If you take this step of emptying yourself and becoming completely and utterly dependent upon Him, you will no longer wonder. Christ set for us an example of complete and total dependence upon His Father and then commanded us to follow in His steps.

> In spite of His eternal equality with the Father...the Lord Jesus for our sakes made Himself nothing (Phil. 2:7 NEB), that the Father might be everything and be glorified in Him! In an attitude of total dependence, He exercised...that perfect "faith-love" relationship for which man by Christ Himself had been created![9]
>
> –IAN THOMAS

Here is the Gospel in a nutshell: "For whosoever will save his life shall lose it; but whosoever shall lose his life for my sake and the gospel's, the same shall save it" (Mark 8:35 KJV). Remember Jia, the 16-year-old Chinese girl who gave up everything for her faith? This verse is the driving theme of her life, and the beauty of Christ cascades through her being.

If you want real beauty, start by trading in all that you are for all that He is. You'll never regret such a glorious exchange.

Sacred Priority
femininity that captivates the masculine heart

3

Cara, a college senior, wants to be transformed by Christ's beauty. But she struggles with a nagging fear. "I know that if I become fully set apart for Christ, I will be beautiful to Him," she said. "But what kind of beauty will make me attractive to a man? How can I win the heart of an earthly prince? If I live a set-apart life for Christ, will I look strange and undesirable to the opposite sex?"

It's all too easy for us to shrink back from the set-apart life because of this fear. We are afraid that if we don't follow pop culture's prescription for feminine allure, we'll never turn a guy's head or win the heart of an earthly prince.

Becoming Attractive to the Right Kind of Guy

I understand where this fear comes from because I felt it myself when I first chose a set-apart life. When we choose Christ's beauty over the world's, we leave ourselves vulnerable to the scornful, misunderstanding gazes of this world, including modern men. Becoming a set-apart young woman—a "lily among thorns"—doesn't mean we become physically unattractive. But it *does* mean that we live differently than the thorns around us, especially when it comes to guys. A set-apart young woman does not seek to win male favor through enhancing her sex appeal or drawing all eyes to her body. She doesn't seek guys' attention through charm, wit, flirting, or manipulation. She doesn't build her life around being noticed by the opposite sex.

Rather, she builds her life around Jesus Christ. And this requires major sacrifice when it comes to scoring male approval because the purity and righteousness that radiates from a set-apart young woman will not appeal to self-focused, sex-obsessed modern men.

The idea of being disregarded or overlooked by guys because we have chosen a different path than other girls can easily make us cringe. It's a thought that can quickly send us running back to the easy, comfortable path of mediocrity.

But we must ask ourselves this question—what kind of guys are we seeking to attract? Do we really want to win the heart of a self-focused man who is only interested in our worldly allure and sex appeal? Or do we want to win the heart of a man who has been captured by Jesus Christ, a guy who sees the priceless value of a woman who shines with His spectacular, radiant loveliness?

Modern manhood, just like modern femininity, is in a sorry state. Most guys have been taught that it's healthy and normal to be obsessed with sex and fixated on the female body. They've been trained to serve their own lustful, selfish desires by cheapening and conquering feminine purity. Even Christian young men are often completely unaware that a higher standard even exists.

But why should we cater to such a debased masculine mentality?

In every generation, there are a few young men who have chosen a different path. They have allowed Jesus Christ to capture their souls and transform their existence into reflections of His glorious strength, honor, and purity. A Christ-built man isn't after a sensuous bikini model who has been shaped and molded by this world's system. Rather, he desires a lily among thorns, a young woman who has been shaped and molded by the loveliness of her heavenly Prince.

The majority of modern guys might not appreciate or value purity and set-apartness. But why would we want a relationship with that kind of man anyway?

If you desire a beautiful, lasting, God-written love story, *hold out for a guy who values the things your heavenly Prince values.*

Before embarking upon the set-apart life, I tried to find fulfillment in relationships—getting married was the end goal. Guys often controlled my sense of happiness. If I had gone a few months without one offer to date, I would begin to lose my sense of contentment. Fear crept in and played with my mind, filling it with dreadful thoughts of never getting married! But God showed me that He alone must be my fulfillment. Today a relationship with a guy is no longer my end goal or pursuit. I truly and wholeheartedly believe that the Lord Jesus will only bring me a guy if it allows me to know Him more. For the first time in my life I can say I am okay with the thought of single life because I can truly say that pursuing more of Jesus Christ is enough. Emptying my life of chick flick movies—those that breed intense discontentment with single life—was one of the biggest helps in coming to this point in my life. Limiting, if not fully removing, the amount of "guy talk" that I engage in with my friends has also greatly helped. The more I allow and make room in my life for Jesus Christ to pursue me, the more He woos me and abundantly fills the void that I once tried to fill with guys.

—Kelly, 24

KRISSY'S STORY (THE CONTINUING SAGA) My sister-in-law, Krissy, chose to set her life apart for Christ at a young age. As an outflow of her devotion to her Prince, she made a decision to live faithfully for her future husband; not to give her heart, emotions, or body away in temporary relationships, but to wait for the man God would one day bring into her life. You may remember Krissy's story of radiant singleness from *Authentic Beauty*. A lot has happened in her life since I wrote that book. Here is the rest of her story.

As Krissy entered her twenties, she still had never been in a relationship. Guys had shown interest in her, but Krissy was holding out for a man whose life was completely centered around Jesus Christ; a man who would not merely appreciate her personality and outward appearance but would be captivated by the supernatural beauty that flowed from the center of her being.

Though she deeply desired to be married and raise a family, Krissy lived her single years entirely focused on Jesus Christ. No matter where she was, she poured out her life for Him, loving and serving everyone around her. She didn't put off living until she finally met her future husband—she lived fully and radiantly each and every day, drawing rich fulfillment and joy from her passionate romance with Jesus Christ. She wasn't obsessed with making herself attractive to the opposite sex. Rather, she was consumed with her heavenly Prince. The only applause that mattered to her was His.

Krissy was (and is) a physically attractive woman. But she did not possess the kind of pop-culture charm that appeals to most modern men. She didn't spend her time and energy becoming more alluring to the world or attractive to guys. Instead, she spent her time and energy serving the poor, teaching small children, going to the mission field, and sharing the Gospel with hurting people. She was marked by the kind of purity and innocence that today's men usually scoff at.

As her twenties passed and she embarked upon her thirties, people began to pressure her to try to snag a guy while she still could. "You should move to a big city where there are more available men," some suggested. "Why don't you start trying a little harder to get guys' attention?" others urged.

It was tempting to listen to these well-meaning words. She wasn't getting any younger, and she longed for an earthly love story. Most of the godly men she met were already married. What if she never met anyone? What if she never got married?

But the gentle words of her Prince resonated through her soul, "Am I enough?"

Even if He never brought a man into her life, Krissy resolved to remain fully set apart for Him. Jesus Christ, not the hope of an earthly romance, was the focus of her existence and the source of her fulfillment. Even without an earthly love story, her heavenly Prince was more than enough. She wasn't living for guys. She wasn't living for an earthly romance. She was living for Him.

One day as Krissy was teaching a Bible study, a young man named Scott walked into the room. He was 36 years old and had never given his heart to a woman. He'd been holding out for a Christ-like princess and waiting faithfully for her all of his life. As he listened to Krissy speak passionately about Jesus Christ, Scott was intrigued. Her eyes shone and her face glowed as she spoke about the Lover of her soul. She seemed completely unconcerned that her overwhelming passion for Christ might make her look or sound foolish to the world. He'd never seen a woman who sparkled with such radiance, such all-consuming love for her heavenly Prince.

Scott came back the next week. And the week after that. Soon, he and Krissy became good friends—drawn together by their mutual love for Christ. And the more he observed of her life, the more fascinated he became. She wasn't like other girls—even other Christian girls. She never changed her personality around him or tried to impress him by saying or doing the right thing. She was far more focused on Christ than she was on trying to turn his head or win his heart.

Krissy possessed a spectacular inner glow that enchanted Scott. The longer he was around her, the more he was drawn to Jesus Christ. After a two-year friendship, Scott asked Krissy to marry him. After much prayer, she said yes. Their friendship and romance was beautiful, tender, sweet, and pure—with Christ always at the center.

At their wedding, I was recruited to sing as Krissy walked down the aisle. As the guests took their seats, the music began and I started my song. But the moment she entered the room in her white wedding dress, radiant and glowing, my throat closed with emotion. No sound would come out. (It didn't help that I could see Eric in the front row, his face contorting with sobs!) The room was flooded with the brilliant presence of God. I could almost see Christ standing there applauding, His eyes beaming with love, and tears of joy glistening on His face as He watched His precious princess walk down the aisle as a sparklingly pure bride.

Krissy had remained faithful and set apart for Him and for her future husband since the age of 12. And today she was receiving His blessing, His reward. That wedding was the most amazing, tender, and supernaturally beautiful ceremony I have ever seen—including my own (which, in my humble opinion, is a very close second!).

Today, Scott and Krissy have three adorable children, a girl and two boys. Her dream of having a family has come true. And yet, the foundation of her existence is still her passionate, ongoing romance with Jesus Christ. He is still her first love and the Lord of her life. And her stunning beauty comes from His radiant life within her.

Finding the Right Guy

Finding a godly guy and experiencing a God-scripted, lasting love story comes down to two simple things:

1. *Build your existence around Christ.* Jesus Christ—not finding the right guy—must be the focus of your life. He must be enough, even if no earthly love story ever comes your way. God may have given you the desire for a beautiful earthly romance, but remember to continually give that dream back to Him and hold it with an open hand, just as Krissy did. Rather than searching for a human love story to meet

your deepest needs for fulfillment and security, find your fulfillment and security in your intimate romance with the Prince of your soul. As beautiful as a God-scripted earthly love story might be, it pales in comparison to the breathtaking romance Jesus Christ desires to have with you, His precious princess. Don't let your longing for human love usurp your longing for more and more of Jesus Christ. As you seek first His kingdom and His righteousness within your life, everything else He desires for you will fall into place in His own perfect time and way (see Matthew 6:33). When He is your first love, you set the stage for a truly amazing God-written earthly romance; one that is merely an extension of the greatest love story of all time.

2. *Be transformed by true beauty.* It's tempting to try to become the kind of sensuous, alluring young woman who turns the heads of modern guys. But as I mentioned before, a Christ-built warrior-poet is not looking for a woman who has been shaped and molded by the world's system. He longs for a woman who has been shaped and molded by the beauty of Jesus Christ. Looking around at the guys in your life, you may not see many, if any, examples of this kind of valiant manhood. But Christ-built guys *do* exist in this generation, and God is raising up more and more of them all the time. If you follow the throngs of self-focused young women in today's world, the likelihood of bumping into a heroic man is slim—because Christ-built guys aren't found at the center of worldly allurements and attractions.

Rather than seeking after his own popularity or self-gratification, a true warrior-poet is busy pouring out his life for his King. He is not chasing after women. He is following hard after Christ. The best way to find a truly Christ-built man is to stop hunting for one and, instead, pour all of your time and energy into your relationship with Jesus Christ. Allow Him to shape you into a lily among thorns. Allow Him to transform you with His radiant beauty; the kind of beauty that will ravish the heart of your King *and* captivate a Christ-built warrior-poet. A set-apart existence may not turn the head of the typical American guy, but it will capture the heart of a Christlike man.

Many generations ago, there lived a beautiful young woman named Sarah. At a very young age, she surrendered her existence to Jesus Christ. He transformed her with His stunning radiance and purity. His lily-white likeness (see Song of Solomon 2:1-2) exuded from her being. As a young teenager, while other girls were focused on finding a husband, Sarah was focused entirely on her romance with her Prince. And as she found her satisfaction and fulfillment in Him, she sparkled with a radiance that caused others to stand back in awe. The following description was written about Sarah by the godly young man who would one day become her husband:

> They say there is a young lady in New Haven who is beloved of that Great Being who made and rules the world. They say that He fills her mind with exceeding sweet delight, and that she hardly cares for anything except to meditate on Him. If you present all the world to her, with the richest of its treasures, she disregards it. She is unmindful of any pain or affliction. She has a singular purity in her affections. You could not persuade her to compromise her true Love even if you would give her all the world. She possesses a wonderful sweetness, calmness, and kindness to those around her. She will sometimes go about from place to place, singing sweetly. She seems to be always full of joy and pleasure, and no one knows exactly why. She loves to be alone, walking in the fields and groves, and seems to have Someone invisible always conversing with her.[1]

Sarah's future husband was enthralled by her all-consuming love for Jesus Christ. It was not worldly allure or charm that captivated the heart of her warrior poet. It was the spectacular loveliness of Christ flowing through her being.

As Sarah and Krissy's lives so beautifully illustrate, it is not the selfish, hollow Maria existence that will draw the heart of a noble knight. It is a woman fully captured by the Lover of her soul, a woman who reflects the stunning loveliness of Jesus Christ.

Sacred Decorum

raising femininity to heavenly heights

4

Carnal Christians profess Christ as their Redeemer, but their actions and decisions are for the sake of their own interests and for who they are in themselves, rather than for God's interests and for who He is. Their minds are still the workshops of the devil, for he can persuade countless numbers of professing Christians to try and be Christians without Christ.[1]

—IAN THOMAS

There are some who would have Christ cheap. They would have Him without the Cross. But the price will not come down.

—SAMUEL RUTHERFORD

Tell me in the light of the Cross, isn't it a scandal that you and I live today as we do?[2]

—ALAN REDPATH

Last week I opened a letter from a distressed college student named Jennifer. "I just can't seem to have intimacy with Jesus in the beautiful way you describe it in your books," she wrote. "I'm sick of living this half-Christian, half-worldly life. I go around saying that I am a Christian, but my Christianity is not based on a passionate relationship with Jesus. I want to find Him, but I don't know how."

How many countless thousands of young women echo Jennifer's despair? Our Christianity is based upon the *idea* of who Christ is, not upon an actual, personal experience with Christ. We may have moments of intimacy with Christ—like during a worship service or reading an inspiring Christian book. But we don't *abide* with Him moment by moment throughout the day. We don't even know how. And if we were to be totally honest, we'd admit that we often feel frustrated with God because He makes Himself so distant. We pray, and He seems not to hear us. We read the Bible, and it is just a blur of spiritual-sounding words. Why, we wonder, does He make being a Christian so difficult? If He really wants a relationship with us, why is He so hard to access?

How can a girl like Jia have such a vibrant relationship with Christ that people stop her on the street to ask why she has such joy, while the rest of us wallow in spiritual mediocrity, doubt, and cynicism?

Christ Himself gave us the answer. "He who has My commandments and keeps them, it is he who loves Me. And he who loves Me will be loved by My Father, and I will love him and manifest Myself to him" (John 14:21).

Jesus Christ reveals Himself to those who follow in His steps. He draws near to those who build their entire lives around His pattern. If we feel far away from Him, it is very likely that we aren't truly building our entire existence around Him; that we are living far more for self than for the glory of His name.

James 1:22 says, "But be doers of the word, and not hearers only, deceiving yourselves." It's not enough to merely read God's Word and esteem it as good. Until we actually begin living out what His Word says, we only deceive ourselves into thinking we are living a real Christian life. We might have a form of godliness, but it has no power to actually *work* in our daily lives (see 2 Timothy 3:5).

I recently heard about a group of young Bible students who were so fed up with modern Christian pretense that they snuck into their campus chapel every Friday night to smoke cigars and gripe for an hour about how pointless the whole Christian existence really was. It was supposed to be "therapy," but at the end of the year, they had gained nothing but slightly diminished lung capacities and seriously diminished faith.

I can't help but wonder what would have happened if they had gone into that campus chapel every Friday night and *prayed*. What if they had decided to really seek God, instead of whining about the fact that He felt so far away? What if they had examined their lives and ruthlessly removed anything and everything that was standing in the way of His power and life overtaking their beings?

We can complain all we want about the fact that God seems distant, but the reality is that He is not far from *anyone* who actually seeks Him (see Acts 17:27). He is ready to manifest Himself to anyone who doesn't just hear His Word, but lives it.

The moment we actually *deny* our self, *pick up our cross,* and *follow* Jesus Christ, as Jia has done, is the moment we are surrounded with the power and presence of His Spirit—not just every once in a while, but every moment of every day.

We might admire women like Amy Carmichael and Gladys Aylward, but we will never showcase that kind of radiant, set-apart femininity unless we are willing to deny ourselves and follow Christ as radically as they did.

There is a sacred decorum of set-apart femininity, a pattern for daily living that marks a young woman as a true daughter of the King. When it comes to our clothes, words, actions, thoughts, pastimes, and pursuits, we must be, as Amy Carmichael put it, "dead to the world and its applause, to all the customs, fashions and laws of those who hate the humbling Cross."[3] We must be consumed with honoring Christ far above meeting our own selfish desires. Not out of duty, but out of delight. Loving Him with such ardor that we *relish* the opportunity to lay everything we possess at His feet. I love how Amy Carmichael expressed it:

> We must look upon the world, with all its delights and all its attractions, with suspicion and reserve. We are called to a higher Kingdom, we are touched with a diviner Spirit. It is not that He forbids us this or that comfort or indulgence; it is not that He is stern, demanding us to follow a narrow path. But we who love our Lord and whose affections are set on Heavenly things voluntarily and gladly lay aside the things that charm and ravish the world, that, for our part, our hearts may be ravished with the things of Heaven that our whole being may be poured forth in constant and unreserved devotion in the service of the Lord who died to save us.[4]

The sacred decorum of a set-apart young woman might be labeled extreme and unnecessary to others, even other Christians. Mary of Bethany lavished her most precious possession upon Christ, pouring every bit of earthly treasure she possessed upon His head. It was an extreme act—a ridiculous outpouring that others viewed as wasteful. But to Christ, it was a beautiful, fragrant offering.

> And while he was at Bethany in the house of Simon the leper, as he was reclining at table, a woman came with an alabaster flask of ointment of pure nard, very costly, and she broke the flask and poured it over his head. There were some who said to themselves indignantly, "Why was the ointment wasted like that? For this ointment could have been sold for more than three hundred denarii and given to the poor." And they scolded her. But Jesus said, "Leave her alone. Why do you trouble her? She has done a beautiful thing to me. For you always have the poor with you, and whenever you want, you can do good for

them. But you will not always have me. She has done what she could; she has anointed my body beforehand for burial. And truly, I say to you, wherever the gospel is proclaimed in the whole world, what she has done will be told in memory of her" (Mark 14:3-9 ESV).

When it comes to pouring out all we possess in radical abandon to the King of all kings, there is no such thing as being too extreme. Nothing we offer to Him out of a heart of loving devotion is ever a wasted sacrifice.

What about *you?* Are you willing to lay aside the things that charm and ravish the world so that your heart may be ravished by the things of heaven? Are you willing to live out the sacred decorum of set-apart femininity even if others label you as extreme?

If you are, prepare to experience the power and presence of God in your life like never before. Prepare to discover a passionate, daily intimacy with Christ that far exceeds your hopes and expectations. Prepare to join the ranks of heroic, set-apart women throughout history.

The answer to Jennifer's heart cry—and the heart cry of countless other disillusioned young Christians—is right here. *If you love Me,* says the gentle whisper of His Spirit, *keep My commandments. Deny yourself, pick up your cross, and follow Me.*

Getting Specific

About two years ago, I heard that gentle whisper as I was sitting in a movie theater. Eric and I were on our "date night." We wanted to spend an evening relaxing and, to put it honestly, go "brain dead" for a couple of hours, to be swept away by the latest Hollywood blockbuster. Of course, we were careful to pick a decent, fairly clean movie that wouldn't fill our minds with a lot of garbage. But then the previews started, and in the space of five minutes, we were exposed to sexual perversion, disgusting bathroom humor, and even outright demonic darkness as the teaser for an upcoming horror movie was shown.

I began to feel uncomfortable. Why was I, as a set-apart child of God, sitting here drinking in such ungodly messages? But then my reasonable side kicked in with a good argument. *God knows I don't agree with all this stuff. I just have to sit through the previews to get to the movie—I didn't ask to see all of this.* I tuned out the still small voice of conviction in my heart as the main movie came onto the screen. I settled down in my seat and prepared to relax and be entertained. But as the movie progressed, the conviction returned. It was a relatively "tame" movie—the instances of cussing and violence were minimal, and the sexual stuff was more "implied" than actually shown. It was a movie that almost every other Christian I know would feel comfortable watching.

But the entire message of the movie was the opposite of God's kingdom. It was the opposite of His nature, His pattern, His ways. It was the opposite of everything that Eric and I stand for and believe. And as we left the theater that night, we began to wonder why we had just spent nearly three hours engaging in something so opposite of the kingdom to which we belong. As we talked about this area of our lives, we were startled to realize just how much of our time, attention, and money was being invested every week into one of the most dark, vile, and ungodly industries in existence.

Hollywood glorifies violence, perversion, and evil. It glamorizes sin and debauchery. It splashes sin across a huge silver screen as an entire culture eagerly drinks in its twisted messages. And yet several times each month, Eric and I were at the video store or the movie theater, ready to participate without even a second thought, ready to give our money to an industry that is the opposite of all that we hold to. Sure, we were careful about the kinds of movies we watched. But even the "milder" ones, for the most part, glorified sin and selfishness. In fact, we struggled to name more than one or two movies we'd ever seen that truly brought honor to the name of Jesus Christ.

I thought about the words of Psalm 1:1-2...

Blessed is the man who walks not in the counsel of the ungodly, nor stands in the path of sinners, nor sits in the seat of the scornful. But his delight is in the law of the LORD, and in His law he meditates day and night.

By clamoring after the world's entertainment and imbibing the images of Hollywood, wasn't I walking in the counsel of the ungodly? By plopping down in a movie theater every week, wasn't I sitting in the seat of the scornful (quite literally, if you think about it) and watching the *very same* garbage as the rest of the world?

By filling my mind and heart with movies and TV, I was certainly not delighting in the law of the Lord and meditating upon it day and night. Rather, I was meditating on the sights, sounds, and messages of pop culture day and night. I was looking to entertainment to bring the rest, refreshment, and pleasure that was supposed to be found in my relationship with Christ. In fact, I started noticing that often when I tried to pray or meditate upon God's word, my mind would be distracted by scenes from a movie or TV show I'd recently seen, and I would have to labor to get my mind back upon heavenly things.

But the idea of giving up my regular "veg out" sessions in front of movies was almost impossible for me to consider. How could I survive without at least a couple hours every few nights each week to relax, unwind, and escape reality? And then the gentle voice of Christ's Spirit reminded me, "A daughter of the King should never have the need to escape reality. In My presence is fullness of joy; at My right hand are pleasures forevermore" (see Psalm 16:11).

I once heard a godly man say that modern Christianity has accepted a counterfeit version of joy and peace by looking to Hollywood and professional sports. We look to movies and television and football games to bring us the pleasure and delight that our King desires to give.[5] And by leaning on worldly entertainment for rest and refreshment, we find only a temporary fix; not lasting happiness or true fulfillment. This was exactly the bait I had fallen for. I had accepted a counterfeit version of peace and joy, and I struggled to believe that I could find something even better in Christ.

When I thought about it, I couldn't picture Elizabeth Fry, Vibia Perpetua, or Gladys Aylward spending every weekend at the movies and rushing out to see *Spiderman Three* on opening night. I couldn't imagine Amy Carmichael or Sabina Wurmbrand getting hooked on *Survivor* or *American Idol.* They were far too busy living out a real-life drama with the King of the universe—spilling out their lives to bring Him glory, reveling in His abundant mercy and faithfulness, marveling at His unspeakable power, and delighting in the joy of His surrounding presence.

But as I pondered taking this step of "laying aside the things that charm and ravish the world," some fears began to arise. Throughout my life, I've encountered many stodgy, rigid, scowling Christians who turned following Christ into a legalistic, stuffy formula. They implied that a Christian was never supposed to have fun or enjoy life. They never even smiled. They seemed to think it was more spiritual to be miserable than to be happy. And they seemed to think that having fun was sinful. It always seemed to be this kind of Christian who believed movies were pure evil, dancing was of the devil, and playing cards was tantamount to witchcraft.

I began to worry…if I traded in my addiction to the world's entertainment for more time with my Bible, wasn't I in danger of becoming like those miserable, dour-faced folks? Wouldn't I become stodgy and legalistic if I let go of the pleasures of pop culture? And for that matter, what would I even *do* in my spare time if I wasn't watching movies or TV?

Some insight from Amy Carmichael helped bring perspective. Though she lived in a time before Hollywood existed, the enticement of pop culture was still there, seeking to lure weak Christians away from complete devotion to Christ. Here is what she had to say about it:

> We often ask the question, "what is the harm of it?"—about reading certain books, following certain pursuits, taking our recreation

in certain ways. Perhaps we have been (working hard) and need a change of thought and rest of brain. What is the harm of the latest novel, even if it happens to be rather unprofitable? And we (who have not the time to read one out of a thousand of the real books that have been written) spend a precious hour by deliberate choice over something not worthwhile. We long to live life to the uttermost, to touch souls to eternal issues. Entire separation to Christ and devotion to Him is required. Is there no other path to reach our goal? There is not. Ours should not be the love that asks, "how little?" but "how much?"; the love that pours out its all and revels in the joy of having anything to pour on the feet of its Beloved. The question "what is the harm?" falls from us and is forgotten when we see Calvary, the Crucified, the risen-again Rabboni of our souls![6]

These words echoed true within the deepest part of my soul. Jesus Christ had given everything for me. Was I not willing to give Him everything in return?

For the past 12 years, Eric and I had challenged our generation not to ask the question "how far is too far?" when it comes to inward and outward purity, but instead to ask "how far can I possibly go to please God and honor my future spouse?" Now, I realized that I needed to stop asking the question "how much can I get away with" when it came to worldly entertainment, and instead ask "how much of my time, energy, money, and attention can I possibly give to the Lord who died to save me?"

As I allowed God's Word to speak to my heart, I realized that asking *that* question would not lead to the stuffy, legalistic, no-fun version of Christianity I was so turned-off by. Rather, it would lead to the dazzling, transforming, radiant beauty of Christ that I longed to exude. It would lead to an even greater depth of sweet intimacy with the Lover of my soul.

When we lay everything at the feet of Jesus and find our deepest fulfillment, rest, peace, strength, and joy in His presence alone—not dulling our spiritual life with worldly counterfeits—we are ushered into the supernatural, superhuman existence God designed us to live. That's when the presence of God draws near. That's when our prayers are heard and answered. That's when the life we read about in Scripture actually becomes our reality.

Most of us constantly battle with the fact that God is distant, intimacy with Christ is difficult to obtain, and our prayers don't seem to be heard. But God says, "You will seek Me and find Me, when you search for Me with all your heart" (Jeremiah 29:13).

Today's young women aren't finding Him because we aren't searching for Him with *all our hearts.* We are too preoccupied with watching reality shows, too busy downloading the latest songs on iTunes, and too enamored with Hollywood's newest production to let our whole beings be poured forth in constant and unreserved devotion in the service of the Lord who died to save us.

Most of us feel we don't have enough time for prayer and seeking God. But we don't even consider giving up our nightly TV time, our weekend movie fests, or our iTunes fetish in exchange for spending time in His presence.

First Timothy 5:6 says, "She who lives in pleasure is dead while she lives." That's a sadly accurate description of today's young Christian woman. Christ-professing modern femininity is steeped in selfish pleasure; pursuing the Maria lifestyle of popularity and worldly applause, pining after the attractions and delights of the culture. And, as a result, we are dead inside. We possess nothing but hollow, propped-up beauty and fake hearts. Christ came so that we might have *life* and have it more abundantly (John 10:10). Building our life around His pattern rather than the world's does not lead to stiff spirituality and legalism. Exchanging counterfeit worldly pleasure for the eternal delights of God's kingdom does not bring misery and death.

It brings *abundant life.* I can say this from firsthand experience.

During the past year and a half of my life, I have never felt so *alive.* Eric and I made a decision to break our addiction to worldly entertainment and instead use our "down time" for prayer, Bible study, and seeking Christ with *all* of our hearts. I know that sounds like exchanging a first-class Caribbean cruise for a year in a prison labor camp. But ironically, it's been the other way around. This step of "pouring out our priceless perfume upon Christ" has led to the most exhilarating season we have ever known. Jesus is more real and intimate than He has ever been. His Word is more powerful and living than it has ever been. Prayer is being heard and miraculously answered as never before. Spending an hour in the presence of God is more refreshing and renewing to me than any Hollywood "mind escape" could ever be.

Of course, this was not an easy step to take. Our sinful, selfish natures screamed and kicked in disapproval in the beginning. Prayer seemed laborious, and we longed for something to coddle our flesh. We even tried to watch Disney movies with our two-year-old son as a way of "escaping and relaxing." But just about the time we decided to offer our entertainment fetish as an offering to our Lord, Hudson decided—completely on his own—that he no longer enjoyed movies. Whenever we tried to turn on *Mary Poppins* or *Herbie,* he would frown and say, "Turn it off pwease!" (God seemed to be helping us break our entertainment fetish.)

Every human rationale presented itself, trying to convince us that such a decision was completely unnecessary and that our relationship with Christ would be just as vibrant spending our night in front of *Pirates of the Caribbean* as it was spending our night in front of His throne.

But now we know better. When we become "dead to the world," we become alive in Christ, and He becomes alive in us. We have tasted and seen that the Lord is good. The question, "would you rather watch a movie tonight or spend some time in prayer?" used to make me laugh. It wasn't even a contest—the movie option *always* won out. I mean, why would I deliberately choose to give up pleasure and fun in exchange for dullness and drudgery? But that was before I really *experienced* that "in His presence is fullness of joy and in His right hand are pleasures forevermore." The pleasure and delight I have discovered in the presence of God have far surpassed any fleeting enjoyment I used to gain from the worldly counterfeit version.

It is something that can only be understood when experienced. I have far greater joy, peace, and heavenly perspective in my daily life. I am far less encumbered by mental distractions and worldly preoccupations. The "self" part of me is not being stroked and coddled and, therefore, I have greater victory over sin on a daily basis. The rest and refreshment He brings are so fulfilling that my controlling need for "down time" in front of movies has completely vanished. A powerful prayer session gives me all the peace, strength, and renewal I could ever want or need. It's truly supernatural. I have no desire to return to where I was before, escaping reality and vicariously living out fake adventures on the big screen. I am far too caught up in the real-life adventure of the set-apart, Christ-infused life. And the real thing is *so* much better than the counterfeit.

> Society and often the church constantly try to tell me that my standards are too high and that my choices are too extreme. But as I devote more of each day to eternal things, I am finding that my desire for earthly distractions and entertainment keeps decreasing and my sense of joy and contentment in the Lord is continually increasing.
>
> –Melanie, 23

Laying Down Idols

"[She] went after her lovers; but Me she forgot," says the LORD (Hosea 2:13).

I realize that this kind of decision sounds radical and ridiculous to most modern Christians. In fact, as I have been writing this chapter, I can just picture the reviews for this book on Amazon: "Leslie's message is outlandish and extreme!" or "Leslie says that all movies are of the devil!" So just to clarify—I do not believe that all movies are evil (though some certainly could not be described any other way. If you have ever seen a horror flick, you know what I mean.) And I do not believe that watching a movie is sinful (unless it is a movie that arouses sinful thoughts and attitudes within you). There are some movies that can even bring glory to God and lead us closer to Him. In the past year, Eric and I watched *Amazing Grace* and were greatly inspired and encouraged by William Wilberforce's incredible devotion to the call of God upon his life. We watched *The Passion* on Easter and were reminded in such a powerful way of Christ's unbelievable act of selfless love for us.

But here is the bottom line. The area of worldly entertainment, for most young Christians, has an unhealthy stranglehold upon us.

As I said in *Authentic Beauty,* one of the ways that you can tell something is an "idol" or "other lover" in your life is that you are *unwilling to let it go;* you can't picture living without it. Most of us, if we were honest, would have to admit that we are unbelievably attached to the world's entertainment. Life would seem empty and bleak if we didn't own a TV. Weekends would be boring and depressing if we didn't frequent the local theater to catch the latest Hollywood flick. Even though we supposedly have everything we could ever want or need in Christ alone, we still look to these other means for the peace, joy, excitement, and refreshment that He Himself desires to give us. All we have is the counterfeit version of peace and joy because we aren't willing to let Him give us the real thing. We are too busy programming our TiVos or buying movie tickets online.

And despite the fact that it is currently hip for pastors to show clips from the latest blockbusters as part of their Sunday sermons, the reality is that movies (or TV shows) that actually bring glory to God and lead us closer to Christ are the *rare exception,* not the rule. When we sit in front of sights, images, and messages that are the opposite of God's kingdom, we allow our minds to be subtly manipulated by the voices of darkness, whether we realize it or not.

I can't even count the number of young women I've met whose favorite movie was the 2004 "chick flick" *The Notebook*. The movie portrays a beautiful romance; showcasing a sweet older couple at the end of their lives who are still passionately in love. It paints a vivid picture of the lifelong love story that we all desire and shows us a man who is so devoted to the love of his life that he stays by her side, tenderly cherishing her, even when she is struck with Alzheimer's and can't remember who he is. The couple dies in each other's arms. What girl wouldn't get teary eyed at such a display? And yet, as the movie flashes back to this couple's younger days, it implies that this kind of beautiful, lifelong love story can be discovered through shallow, sensual attraction, animalistic pre-marital sex, rebellion against parents, breaking of promises, and betrayal of trust.

Not only are the sex scenes in this movie lengthy and graphic, they portray a patently false and dangerous message. There is no way to discover Christlike, lasting love without following Christ's pattern. Build a relationship the way that couple did, and I guarantee you are going to end up with heartache, bitterness, and misery, not the "happily ever after" ending you see in the movie. But *The Notebook* makes sin seem so right, so good, and so noble. When sin is so beautifully and artistically portrayed, it's easy to allow Hollywood moviemakers to subtly shape our thinking, even on a subconscious level. *Look at how well their love story turned out,* we start reasoning, *and they had sex before marriage. It was so sweet and beautiful; I can't imagine that it was wrong. They were just following their hearts! Maybe I shouldn't be so uptight about this whole purity thing after all.*

One young woman I talked to, after seeing a handful of movies that portrayed affairs as beautiful and right (rather than selfish and sinful), became convinced that it was okay for people to leave their marriage partner for someone else if they found their "soul mate."

I can't help but wonder why we as Christ-professing young women are so willing to submit our minds and emotions to an industry that openly mocks the purity and righteousness of our heavenly Prince.

Most of us are far more influenced by pop culture than we are by the Word of God. We can quote our favorite lines from a hundred different chick flicks, but the only Scripture we know is John 3:16.

And we wonder why Christ feels distant.

But it's not just movies and TV that have us in their controlling vise. It's an overall preoccupation with pop culture. Music artists, professional athletes, and movie stars claim far more of our applause and attention than Jesus Christ does.

"Little children, keep yourselves from idols" are the closing words that sum up the entire book of First John (1 John 5:21). Idols are not just golden statues that people bow down to in ornate temples. An idol is anything that claims our attention and affection above Christ. Most of us verbally declare that Jesus Christ is more important to us than our fetishes for music or movies. But what do our lives say? Where do we spend the best hours of our days? What do we turn to for enjoyment and comfort?

> A pure heart is one to which all that is not of God is strange and jarring.
>
> —John Tavler

Pop culture floods our minds and senses with things that are not of God. But for most of us, the glamorized sin that surrounds us is not strange and jarring. It's normal and accepted. In fact, we go out of our ways to enjoy and participate in it. We even spend a huge amount of our time and money on it. And we allow it to capture our minds, emotions, and attention.

Many of us have seen pastors or Christian authors rely on movies (rather than God's Word) to illustrate his or her point. Because Hollywood can so poignantly and artistically capture human angst and emotion, it is all too easy to "spiritualize" movies, blending ungodly messages in with our pursuit of godly truth. But God's truth will not be discovered through profane images, no matter how profound Hollywood's messages might seem.

Remember that cult leader who gave his followers Kool-Aid to drink, and they all died? Kool-Aid by itself is harmless enough. It's a sweet, refreshing beverage that can be safely enjoyed even by kids. But when Kool-Aid is mixed with poison, it changes from a harmless beverage into a deadly toxin. In the same way, when truth is mingled with the poisonous ideas of Hollywood, it brings about death, not life.

> For what fellowship has righteousness with lawlessness? And what communion has light with darkness? And what accord has Christ with Belial? Or what part has a believer with an unbeliever? And what agreement has the temple of God with idols? (2 Corinthians 6:14-15).

A Christian young woman I know recently told me that she didn't think her obsession with *American Idol* was wrong, despite the fact that the very title of the show promotes idolatry. She was convinced that she could see God's nature somewhere amidst all the hype, human glory, and celebrity worship.

Pretending that God showcases His truth or His nature through ungodly channels is just a clever excuse for participating in worldly allurements. Scripture makes it very clear that our Holy King is not found amidst worldly glitz or man-made fame. He does not share His glory with men or idols.

> I am the LORD, that is My name. And My glory I will not give to another, nor My praise to carved images (Isaiah 42:8).

> Professing to be wise, they became fools, and changed the glory of the incorruptible God into an image made like corruptible man (Romans 1:22-23).

Christ makes it clear that we cannot love both Him *and* the things that charm and ravish this world. We cannot be dazzled by the images of pop culture *and* captivated by the King of all kings.

> Do not love the world or the things in the world. If anyone loves the world, the love of the Father is not in him. For all that is in the world—the lust of the flesh, the lust of the eyes, and the pride of life—is not of the Father but is of the world (1 John 2:15-16).

> Adulterers and adulteresses! Do you not know that friendship with the world is enmity with God? Whoever therefore wants to be a friend of the world makes himself an enemy of God (James 4:4).

The set-apart women of history past were not only willing to give up all the pleasures and enticements of the world for His sake, but they poured out everything they held precious upon Him without reserve, like Mary of Bethany. (Sabina Wurmbrand was even willing to sacrifice her beloved husband and child for the glory of Christ.)

A truly set-apart woman is marked by this sacred decorum. She hates the things that God hates and loves the things that God loves, and she reflects this attitude in every dimension of her daily life. Does God stand up and cheer over *American Idol?* Does He smile with delight over the new Harry Potter movie? Does He get excited about the latest Coldplay album?

Or does He grieve over our distracted, wandering, divided hearts?

If our Lord does not take delight in the things that charm and ravish the world, neither should we. (And if you believe that God actually applauds the distorted messages of pop culture, you need to become better acquainted with the God of the Bible.)

Other "Christian" girls may watch the same movies, listen to the same music, wear the same clothes, and have all the same pop-culture addictions as the rest of the world with just slightly higher morals tacked on. But God has called *us* to a higher standard—the very standard of Christ. And I believe it's time we become worthy of the calling we have received.

Becoming His Temple

Becoming a Christian is a lot more than just saying a sinner's prayer and gaining the assurance that we'll go to heaven someday. It is a sacred exchange. It means entering into a holy, eternal covenant with the King of all kings. It's a giving up of all that we have and all that we are in exchange for all that He has and all that He is. When we invite Christ into our life, we don't "make room" for Him amidst our selfishness, sin, and worldly pursuits. Rather, by the power of His grace, we are transformed and made completely new—adorned with His spectacular beauty, like the woman in Ezekiel. Our bodies actually become the dwelling place of Almighty God—we house His very Spirit within us. And His temple is not to be defiled:

> Or do you not know that your body is the temple of the Holy Spirit who is in you, whom you have from God, and you are not your own? For you were bought at a price; therefore glorify God in your body and in your spirit, which are God's (1 Corinthians 6:19-20).

> For now have I chosen and sanctified this house, that my name may be there for ever. And mine eyes and mine heart shall be there perpetually (2 Chronicles 7:16 KJV).

> How lovely is Your dwelling place, O LORD Almighty! (Psalm 84:1 NIV).

Before Christ came to this earth, the Jewish temple was where the presence of God dwelt. Keeping the temple immaculate, beautiful, and consecrated for Him was such a serious and holy task that it occupied every thought and action of every Jewish priest throughout his entire life. Once a year, one high priest was chosen to enter the Holy of Holies—the chamber that housed the very presence of God. With holy dread and trembling, the priest would meticulously repent of every speck of unrighteousness, offering sacrifices for even the minutest of sins in his heart. Then he would enter the holy place with a rope tied around his ankle in case he was struck dead in the presence of God and his body needed pulling out. Jewish legend said that if this priest allowed even one sinful thought into his mind while in the Holy of Holies, the entire world could be destroyed.[7] The temple of God was serious business because it housed the very presence of the Almighty.

And now, *we* are the temple of God. *We* house the very presence of the Almighty. Should we be cavalier and haphazard with a task that was once the most sacred of all? The seriousness with which the temple was treated in the Old Testament reveals the seriousness of our position as Christ's temple now. That means we are to be holy as He is holy. We are to be vigilantly on guard against any unclean word, thought, action, or attitude that would dare defile His sacred temple. To become the holy dwelling place of the Most High is the essence of true set-apartness:

> For you are the temple of the living God. As God has said: "I will dwell in them and walk among them. I will be their God, and they shall be My people. Therefore come out from among them and be separate," says the Lord. "Do not touch what is unclean, and I will receive you" (2 Corinthians 6:16-17).

Scripture is very clear about what it means to be the holy temple of God. We are not to mix darkness with light. We are not to touch what is unclean. We are to be, as Amy Carmichael put it, "completely separate in spirit from the world and wholly devoted to Christ."

But most of us prefer to take those verses as "allegorical" instead of letting them influence our practical, real-life, day-to-day decisions.

Proverbs 30:20 (NKJV) says, "This is the way of an adulterous woman: she eats and wipes her mouth, and says, 'I have done no wickedness.'" What a sadly accurate picture of modern Christian femininity! We feast upon the delights and attractions of this world, then wipe our mouths and coyly declare that we have done nothing wrong. We devote our hearts, minds, and bodies to chasing after "other lovers." Meanwhile, we have left our first Love. We justify our spiritual adultery with clever-sounding arguments about needing to be "in touch with the culture" so that we can win others to Christ. We convince ourselves that to understand the angst of sinners, we need to participate in their sin right along with them.

Just this week, an influential Christian woman told us, "Your message is way too extreme. Jesus fit into the world. He was attractive to the world so that people could identify with Him. We as Christians need to be attractive to the world and even look like the world at times. After all, God isn't calling us to be Quakers!" (I am assuming that, to this woman, the verse "come out from among them and be separate, and touch not the unclean thing" means something different than what it actually says. I am also assuming that she knows very little about the many amazing, Christ-honoring Quakers throughout the years who have impacted history for the kingdom of God, such as Elizabeth Fry.)

I once heard a pastor say that we should watch several hours of TV each week so that we make sure to stay in touch with the thoughts and agendas of the world. I can't help but wonder whether this same pastor ever encouraged his people to spend several hours in prayer each week to stay in touch with the thoughts and agendas of God's Spirit.

As the younger generation, we intrinsically shy away from words like "holiness" or "righteousness" because they smack of the dour-faced, rigid, legalistic spirituality of generations past. Coming out from the world and being separate makes us think of joining an Amish society or a nunnery. So instead of taking God at His word, we conveniently overlook the Scriptures that challenge us to a set-apart life, all because we are afraid of falling into the trap of legalism. But the "fear of legalism" is often just an excuse to keep living self-ruled, pleasure-seeking, sin-loving lives.

Legalism is merely the futile attempt to do in our own strength what the Spirit of God means to accomplish *on our behalf.* Remember those words from Oswald Chambers? "We are to be perfect as He was perfect. Not by striving and effort, but by the *impartation of that which is Perfect.*" The reason that dour-faced, super-stiff Christians are so miserable and so bound to countless rules is that they are striving in their own might to live righteously before God. They have never yielded to the supernaturally enabling power of God to work in and through them, enabling them to live a truly miraculous set-apart life that is not propped up by human effort. Their Christianity is dead.

But so is ours. We have retaliated against legalistic Christianity by swinging the opposite direction, mocking the idea of holiness and trying to be as much like the world as possible in order to prove that Christianity isn't just for stuffy librarians and backwoodsy country schoolmarms.

God requires His sons and daughters to live by a sacred decorum, to come out from the world and be separate, to touch not the unclean thing. We are to ruthlessly remove all uncleanness, envy, jealousy, idolatry, filthy talk, perverted joking, and sexual compromise from our lives. As set-apart young women, there is not even to be a hint of these things in our daily existence:

> But fornication and all uncleanness or covetousness, let it not even be named among you, as is fitting for saints; neither filthiness, nor foolish talking, nor coarse jesting, which are not fitting, but rather giving of thanks. For this you know, that no fornicator, unclean person, nor covetous man, who is an idolater, has any inheritance in the kingdom of Christ and God (Ephesians 5:3-5).

How do we live this kind of holy, upright, God-honoring life? Not by instigating rules and formulas for ourselves. Not by joining a nunnery or becoming a backwoods hermit. Rather, by yielding to the transforming, supernaturally enabling power of Christ in us. By allowing Him to completely remake us from the inside out. By submitting ourselves fully and completely to His transforming work. By laying our selfish pursuits and worldly addictions upon the altar at His feet.

When we yield our bodies to become the holy, undefiled dwelling places of the Most High God, He comes and makes His home within us. When we allow Him to remove everything carnal, sinful, and selfish that stands in the way, that's when His spectacular beauty can shine unhindered through our beings.

> If anyone cleanses himself from what is dishonorable, he will be a vessel for honorable use, set apart as holy, useful to the master of the house, ready for every good work (2 Timothy 2:1 ESV).

> How lovely is Your dwelling place, O LORD Almighty! (Psalm 84:1 NIV).

One of my biggest challenges to living a set-apart life in today's culture is the constant barrage of worldly and fleshly things: secular music blasting in stores, checkout stands littered with magazines promoting celebrity gossip, diet tips, and the latest fashion demands, and even TVs in public places that try to distract and invade my mind. Matthew 6:22 (KJV) says, "If therefore thine eye be single, thy whole body shall be full of light." I constantly must choose to turn my eyes from worthless and destructive things and set my gaze on heavenly things. I've found it very helpful to listen to Scripture on my iPod as I get ready each day.

And instead of listening to music in the car, I use that valuable time alone to spend with God in prayer. The more I practice turning from pop culture and dwelling instead upon the truths and treasures of Jesus Christ, the appeal of these worldly things grows dimmer and dimmer in light of His glorious life!

–Annie, 25

Come Away—Making It Practical

If you are ready to step into the sacred decorum of set-apart femininity, here are some practical ways to begin.

Live for Him Alone

I recently read a speech given by a Jewish father at his son's bar mitzvah. He exhorted his son not to apologize for being Jewish, but to unapologetically embrace the holy calling upon his life.

> To be holy is to be different. That which is holy is set apart. What is a Jew? It is the courage to be different. While the rest of the world strives to be loved, the Jew strives to be holy. While the rest of the world strives to impress their fellow man, the Jew strives to impress none but God alone.[8]

A set-apart young woman has the courage to be different. It has been said, "He [or she] who fears God fears no man."[9] While other young women strive to be noticed and accepted by the world, the set-apart young woman cares for no opinion but God's. Most of us spend an incredible amount of time and effort trying to explain away the holy calling upon our lives, rather than unapologetically embracing it and allowing God to accomplish this profound miracle in and through us.

To join the ranks of set-apart women throughout history, it is critical that we lay down our cravings for the world's approval. When we become the holy temple of the living God, we will not be understood or accepted by the sinful, carnal world around us. In fact, if we are applauded and approved by secular society (like Maria), in all likelihood we are not truly allowing the Spirit of God to fully own and operate us. Jesus said, "If the world hates you, you know that it hated Me before it hated you. If you were of the world, the world would love its own. Yet because you are not of the world, but I chose you out of the world, therefore the world hates you" (John 15:18-19).

And it makes me sad to say this, but the scorn we receive might not only come from unbelievers. If we embrace the sacred decorum of set-apart femininity, it is probable that many of our fellow Christians will look at us with a sketchy eye. That's because modern Christianity, by and large, is far more concerned about impressing the world than being consumed with Christ alone. The popularity of seeker-sensitive mega-churches—where Bibles are left at home in exchange for fancy Starbucks drinks and kids play Xbox games during Sunday school—is just one example of how the modern church has watered down the Christ-life to nothing more than joining a social club.

And when we choose a different path, it makes them uncomfortable. Two college-aged young women who recently attended one of our Authentic Girl conferences returned home to eagerly share with their Bible study group how God was challenging them to live lives radically abandoned to Jesus Christ. Instead of being excited and supportive, the other members of the group asked them never to come back—even though it was a group the two girls had started in the first place. Sadly, such stories are not uncommon. Every week it seems, I hear from another young woman who, simply because she has chosen to pursue Jackie's version of femininity instead of Maria's, has been labeled "outlandish and extreme" by her close Christian friends.

Don't be discouraged or derailed by the scorn of the world or the disregard of mediocre Christians. Rather, if you find yourself the target of criticism for Christ's sake, rejoice in the realization that you are on the right track. Remember that "all who desire to live godly in Christ Jesus will suffer persecution" (2 Timothy 3:12). Every set-apart woman who has made a dent in world history walked this path.

Esther Ahn Kim was labeled an inconsiderate selfish troublemaker by her Christian coworkers when she refused to obey governmental orders to bow to the "sun god" at a Japanese shrine. Gladys Aylward was called a foolish, irresponsible risk taker when she chose to obey God's call to take His Word to China, and no missionary society would support her. Sabina Wurmbrand was treated as the scum of society—by Christians and unbelievers alike—when she took a stand against the Communist agenda to protect the name of Christ. Amy Carmichael was so disliked by her fellow Christian missionaries that they made a concerted effort to run her out of India. And when Vibia Perpetua decided to give her life for Christ and let her child be raised by another, her family heaped guilt and condemnation upon her.

Don't expect a round of human applause when you choose the set-apart life. But remember that in its place you will gain something far better—a standing ovation from Jesus Christ. I love the story of Stephen heroically giving his life for the sake of the Gospel. Just before he died, he saw heaven opened and the Son of Man *standing* at the right hand of the Father (see Acts 7:56). Stephen's willing sacrifice brought such delight to the heart of Christ that the King of all kings actually *stood* to welcome him into eternity. I don't know about you, but that's all the applause I could ever want or need.

Silence Your Selfish Side

In every moment of every day, we have one of two choices to make. We can either listen to our selfish whims and wants, or listen to the Spirit of Christ within us. Our selfish sides are what are referred to in Scripture as our "flesh." There is a continual battle between our flesh and the Spirit of God. Whatever the Spirit of God desires, our flesh automatically rebels against. That's why we are told to *put to death* our fleshly whims and desires and yield only to the Spirit's commands:

> For if you live according to the flesh you will die; but if by the Spirit you put to death the deeds of the body, you will live (Romans 8:13).

> Let us invite the searching eye of God to locate this corrupted, spotted, stinking Self in us. Let it be torn from us and "crucified with Him, so that henceforth we no longer serve sin" (see Romans 6:6).[10]
>
> —LEONARD RAVENHILL

This morning when my alarm went off, I instantly had a choice to make. Should I yield to the beckoning whisper of my Prince asking me to get up and spend time with Him or listen to my own selfish desire to stay in bed? My entire day is filled with those kinds of decisions. I can either claim my life as my own and do what my flesh desires, or I can submit my entire existence to Him. The more I yield to His Spirit, the more I am able, by His supernatural grace, to live the set-apart life He has called me to live.

Someone speaks rudely to me. Do I snap back sarcastically, as my flesh desires, or do I surrender to Christ and let His love season my response? A family member does something hurtful. Do I revel in my right to be angry and bitter, as my flesh insists, or do I yield to Christ and let His forgiveness flow through me? I have an hour free at the end of a long day. Do I use it for my own pleasure, as my flesh tells me to, or do I find true refreshment in the presence of my King?

Daily life is filled with hundreds of choices to either give in to selfish whims or yield to Christ's Spirit. But most of us are so used to obeying the commands of our carnal desires that our ears are deaf to the Spirit of God. Silencing our selfish sides takes a lot of focus and a heavy dose of supernatural enabling grace. But Christ is more than interested in equipping us to put to death the desires of our flesh.

When you woke up this morning, did you think of your day as belonging to you or Him? Did you live as if your time and decisions were your own or His? Did you allow the distractions and allurements of this world to turn your head, to occupy your thoughts, or to dictate your choices? Or was He your sole pursuit?

If you are like most modern young women, you probably have selfish habit patterns that need to be remade by Christ's Spirit. I would encourage you to spend some focused time in prayer and waiting on God, allowing Him to gently reveal those areas of your life that need His transforming touch. Allow His Spirit to open your eyes to any part of your daily existence in which you typically yield to your selfish whims and desires. You may find it helpful to write down anything that He brings to mind. Then pray specifically for the grace to silence your selfish side in each of these areas and begin putting it into practice in your everyday life. (For example, choose to joyfully respond when your alarm clock goes off instead of lazily pushing the snooze button or angrily hurling it across the room.)

It may take a few days, weeks, or months for those old habits to fully die. But if you allow Him to retrain and enable you to "deny yourself, pick up your cross, and follow Him," you will soon understand from firsthand experience what Paul meant when he said, "it is no longer I who live, but Christ who lives in me" (Galatians 2:20).

Come Away with Him

When I married Eric, I took on his name. I became Mrs. Eric Ludy. (I could lament about the misfortune of being stuck with Ludy for a last name, but that is beside the point.) I took on Eric's name to solidify my marriage covenant with him. It wasn't just accepting the title "Mrs. Eric Ludy"—it was a total change of focus and lifestyle.

> My Beloved spoke and said unto me: "Rise up, my love, my fair
> one, and come away" (Song of Solomon 2:10).

What would be the point of taking on the name Ludy if I didn't change my life after the wedding? What if, after the vows were spoken, I went back to my own house, slept alone in my own bed, and went about my daily life as if I were still single? Bearing Eric's name meant *building my life* around my new name.

To truly bear the name of my husband—not just in title, but in my daily reality—I had to leave my own life behind and join my groom in a *new* life. I had to become one with him.

To become a true *Christian*—the one who bears the name of Jesus, our beloved Bridegroom—we must leave behind our own lives and come away with Him. We must put aside all of our own selfish desires and pursuits. He must become the sole focus and worship of our lives. As it says in Psalm 45:10-11, "Listen, O daughter. Consider and incline your ear. Forget your own people also, and your father's house; so the King will greatly desire your beauty. Because He is your Lord, worship Him." And as Henry Blackaby said, "You cannot stay where you are and go with God."[11]

I love this statement from Charles Spurgeon:

> Jesus says, "Rise up, my love, my fair one and come away." He asks you to come out from the world and be separate and touch not the unclean thing. Make no reserves. Come altogether away from selfishness—from anything which would divide your chaste and pure love to Christ—your soul's Husband. Come away from your old habits. Avoid the very appearance of evil. Come away from old friendships which may tempt you back to the flesh pots of Egypt. Leave all these things. Come away to private communion. Come away, shut the doors of your chamber and talk with your Lord Jesus and have close and intimate dealing with Him. Oh, take care that you begin aright by coming right away from the world, by making your dedication perfect, complete, unreserved, sincere, spotless.

Our precious Bridegroom is calling us, beckoning us to leave all behind and come away with Him. This is not just a theoretical request—it is a practical one. We must ask ourselves what in our lives is keeping us from being consumed by Him alone. Is it our habits of laziness? Our selfish attitudes? Our addictions to worldly entertainment? Our thirst for comfort and material possessions? Our desires to be appealing to the opposite sex? Our longing to be center stage? Our need for control over our own futures? Our need for popularity and attention? Our fascination with pop culture?

Sophie is a college freshman who told me about a recent struggle in her relationship with Christ. "All my life I dreamed of being in a sorority," she confessed. "But when I finally got into one, I noticed that all of the conversations and attitudes of the other girls were completely opposite of Christ. They were completely preoccupied with worldly things. And I found that I was becoming preoccupied with all the same things."

Sophie had a difficult decision to make. Should she walk away from her lifelong dream just because the sorority made it somewhat more difficult for her to focus on Christ? Other Christians in her life said she was being extreme and ridiculous. "Being a part of a sorority is an experience you'll never forget," they told her. "Why would you give it up? All of the preoccupation with guys and clothes and parties is just harmless fun. You only go to college once! And besides, think of the great witness for Christ you can be in that environment."

But when Sophie listened to the voice of her King, He spoke a different message. He softly beckoned her to "come away."

"I went back and forth about it for weeks," she admitted. "But I read something in *Authentic Beauty* that helped open my eyes: *If any pastime, activity, habit, relationship, or friendship in your life tends to pull you away from Christ, that's a sign that it doesn't belong in your life.* I finally realized that nothing in the world is worth jeopardizing my relationship with Christ. A sorority is a stupid, meaningless thing that lasts for a couple years. My relationship with Christ is the most precious and valuable part of my life—it's the only thing that matters—and it lasts for eternity. So I walked away. It made no sense to anyone else. But now, I am closer to Him than I ever dreamed possible. Before, He was just a part of my life. Now, He *is* my life."

What about you? Is Jesus Christ merely a part of your life? *Or is He your entire life?*

We each have our own sororities—dreams, activities, or pastimes that distract us from our one true Love. When Christ says, "Rise up and come away," He is asking if we, like Sophie, are willing to walk away from those things—to leave them far behind—and ride off into the sunset in the arms of our precious Prince.

This "coming away" from the world must apply to every dimension of our lives as set-apart young women; areas such as music, entertainment, dress, and language. Take some time to think and pray through each of the following areas of your own life, allowing God's Spirit to gently reveal any worldly attitudes or patterns that need to be transformed by His grace.

> Are there chambers of the mind with unclean pictures hanging in them? Have we skeletons in the cupboards of our hearts? Can the Holy Ghost be invited to take us by the hand down the corridors of our souls? Are there not secret springs, and secret motives that control, and secret chambers where polluted things hold empire over our soul?[12]
>
> —Leonard Ravenhill

> Search me, O God, and know my heart. Try me, and know my thoughts. And see if there be any wicked way in me, and lead me in the way everlasting (Psalm 139:23-24 KJV).

Entertainment Questions:

- Have I been surrendering my mind and emotions to Hollywood's ungodly messages?

- Do I watch movies and shows that glorify darkness or perversion, mock God, or make sin seem noble, even in subtle ways?

- Do I justify my participation in Hollywood's ungodly messages? (Hint: If you catch yourself thinking things like, *As long as I don't agree with the bad stuff in this movie, it's okay for me to watch it,* or *This movie has a good message if I just ignore the sex and profanity,* or *Every other Christian I know would watch this movie, and it's only rated PG-13, so it's probably fine,* then it's time to let Christ reshape your standards.)

- Do I turn to TV or movies for a counterfeit version of rest, refreshment, and enjoyment instead of going to Christ for the real thing?

- Am I addicted to movies or TV shows? (Hint: If you are unwilling or unable to go without these things, that's a sign they have an unhealthy hold on your life.)

- Am I willing to use the time I would normally spend being entertained by Hollywood to further my prayer life and deepen my relationship with Christ?

- Are there any practical changes that Christ's Spirit is asking me to make (by His enabling grace) in this area of my life?

Music Questions:

- Do I listen to music that glorifies darkness or perversion, mocks God, or makes sin seem noble, even in subtle ways?

- Do I justify my participation in the ungodly messages of secular music? (Hint: If you catch yourself thinking things like, *As long as I don't agree with the bad stuff in this song, it's okay for me to listen to it,* or *This song has a really good message even though it's written by a darkness-loving, sexually twisted, alcoholic drug addict,* then it's time to let Christ reshape your standards.)

- Do I idolize any music artist or music group? (And remember this applies to both secular *and* Christian artists. At a Christian music festival Eric and I spoke at, a Christian "guy band" emerged onto the stage amidst hysterical cheers from thousands of Christ-professing young women. After a couple of hip-swiveling tunes, the singers wiped their sweaty faces with towels and then threw them into the crowd of girls, who clawed and fought over the towels in an idol-worshipping frenzy. The irony of the whole scene was that a banner hung over the stage with the words, "A Tribute to Our Creator.")

- Am I addicted to music? (Hint: If you are unwilling or unable to go without it, that's a sign that it has an unhealthy hold on your life.)

- Am I willing to use the time I would normally spend downloading songs from iTunes to further my prayer life and deepen my relationship with Christ?

- Are there any practical changes that Christ's Spirit is asking me to make (by His enabling grace) in this area of my life?

Note: Just as with movies, I am not trying to imply that enjoying music is bad or that listening to a secular song is sinful. But it is crucial that music never becomes an idol in our lives, and that we do not allow the ungodly messages of the secular music industry to shape any aspect of our lives. As with all other areas, this is an arena that Christ must have full reign over.

Internet Questions:

- Do I visit Internet sites that glorify darkness or perversion, mock God, or make sin seem noble, even in subtle ways?

- Do I allow the Internet to influence me toward materialism, idolatry, or pop-culture preoccupation?

- Do I use the Internet (Internet dating sites, chat rooms, and so forth) as a form of selfish control or manipulation in the area of guy/girl relationships?

- Do I use sites like MySpace or Facebook to draw attention to myself, gain popularity, or be noticed by the opposite sex? (Note: Having a blog or personal web page might not be harmful in itself, but be sure to examine your heart's motives and your method of presentation first. Make sure it truly brings glory to God and not merely attention to you. Also consider the *kind* of site you are endorsing by participating in it. Does it glorify God or glorify sin and selfishness?)

- Am I addicted to the Internet? (Hint: If you are unwilling or unable to give it up, that's a sign it has an unhealthy hold on your life.)

- Am I willing to use the time I would normally spend online to further my prayer life and deepen my relationship with Christ?

- Are there any practical changes that Christ's Spirit is asking me to make (by His enabling grace) in this area of my life?

Magazine Questions:

- Do I read magazines that glorify darkness or perversion, mock God, or make sin seem noble, even in subtle ways?

- Do I allow magazines to influence me toward materialism, idolatry, or pop-culture preoccupation?

- Do I allow magazines to define feminine allure and make me preoccupied with my own body, my own style, and my own external beauty?

- Am I addicted to magazines? (Hint: If you are unwilling or unable to give it up, that's a sign it has an unhealthy hold on your life.)

- Am I willing to use the time I would normally spend reading secular magazines to further my prayer life and deepen my relationship with Christ?

- Are there any practical changes that Christ's Spirit is asking me to make (by His enabling grace) in this area of my life?

Book Questions:

- Do I read books or novels that glorify darkness or perversion, mock God, or make sin seem noble, even in subtle ways?

- Do I allow books or novels to influence me toward materialism, idolatry, or pop-culture preoccupation?

- Do I allow romance novels to define my perspective on relationships or make me discontent with singleness?

- Do I lean upon novels to bring the rest, refreshment, and enjoyment that Christ wants to give me?

- Am I addicted to books or novels? (Hint: If you are

unwilling or unable to give it up, that's a sign it has an unhealthy hold on your life.)

- Do I allow Christian books to take the place of really digging into God's Word?
- Am I willing to use the time I would normally spend reading novels to further my prayer life and deepen my relationship with Christ?
- Are there any practical changes that Christ's Spirit is asking me to make (by His enabling grace) in this area of my life?

Language Questions:

- Does my daily speech reflect the holy nature of Christ?
- Do I allow crude or coarse joking, vulgarity, or profanity to come out of my mouth?
- Do I allow criticism, gossip, slander, or cruel words to come out of my mouth?
- Are there any practical changes that Christ's Spirit is asking me to make (by His enabling grace) in this area of my life?

...neither filthiness, nor foolish talking, nor coarse jesting, which are not fitting, but rather giving of thanks (Ephesians 5:4).

No man can tame the tongue. It is an unruly evil, full of deadly poison. With it we bless our God and Father, and with it we curse men, who have been made in the similitude of God. Out of the same mouth proceed blessing and cursing. My brethren, these things ought not to be so (James 3:8-10).

Clothing Questions:

- Do I wear clothes that draw attention to the sensual parts of my body?

- Do I use seductive clothes to gain the approval and notice of guys?

- Do I wear clothes that glorify rebellion, darkness, or perversion?

- Am I addicted to the trends and fashions of pop culture?

- Do I lean upon clothes and style for identity and security?

- Do I spend an unhealthy amount of time, energy, and money maintaining my wardrobe?

- Are there any practical changes that Christ's Spirit is asking me to make (by His enabling grace) in this area of my life?

  (Note: There is nothing "spiritual" about wearing dowdy, unattractive clothing. In fact, the Proverbs 31 woman seems to have an incredible sense of dignity and style. However, like all the other areas we have been discussing, it is vital that we follow the Spirit of God rather than the messages of the culture when choosing what to wear. Our clothing choices should be an outward reflection of the beauty, radiance, joy, and purity that Christ has built within our inner life. Personally, I love dressing with elegance and style—and it is something that Eric appreciates as well. But if I ever find myself obsessing over my wardrobe or lowering my standards for modesty just to stay up with current trends, that's when I know God needs to remake my habits in this area.)

Activities and Pastimes:

- Do I engage in any activities or pastimes that lead me further away from Jesus Christ?

- Do I engage in any activities or pastimes that glorify darkness, perversion, or sin, even in subtle ways?

- Do I engage in any activities or pastimes that awaken or stroke my selfish, fleshly nature and diminish the Spirit-life of Christ?

- Do I spend my free time pursuing selfish, fleshly cravings rather than cultivating my relationship with Jesus Christ?

- Am I addicted to (or unwilling to give up) any activity or pursuit?

- Are there any practical changes that Christ's Spirit is asking me to make (by His enabling grace) in these areas of my life?

Friendships:

- Do I have any friendships that lead me further away from Jesus Christ?

- Do I have any friends who influence me toward darkness, perversion, or sin, even in subtle ways?

- Do I have any friends who awaken or stroke my selfish, fleshly nature and diminish the Spirit-life of Christ?

- Are there any unhealthy, ungodly friendships in my life that I need to walk away from?

   (Note: Being friends with unbelievers or mediocre Christians is fine, especially if you are able to have a positive, godly influence upon them. But whenever a friendship is pulling you away from Jesus Christ or leading you toward sin, it's time to walk away from it, no matter how difficult it may be (see 2 Corinthians 6:14).

To live life daily pursuing Jesus Christ above all else requires the emptying of anything that stands in the way. The largest obstacle for me was time. How would I find the time to study the Word of God and then go and live it? Though I could not empty my life of required responsibilities, such as work and school, I could choose to use my free time differently. I used to spend my free time consuming media—visiting movie theaters, watching television, skimming through magazines, surfing the Internet, and attending concerts. The Lord Jesus challenged me with Psalm 16:11. He asked me to empty myself of all of these things that I thought would bring me pleasure and, instead, use my free time to be filled with the things that edify, promote, and deepen my relationship with Him. The results were an abundance of time that I never knew existed and the beginning of an ever-deepening relationship with Jesus Christ—bringing me more joy and pleasure than I could have dreamed of!

—Kelly, 24

Finding True Pleasure

We cannot expect an intimate, passionate daily relationship with Christ if we are not willing to seek Him with *all* our hearts, souls, minds, and strength. When we are preoccupied with pop culture and the pursuit of our own selfish pleasures, we cannot truly know Him or hear His voice. But when we, like Mary of Bethany, are willing to pour out everything we hold dear upon the precious head of our beloved without reserve, we will experience firsthand that "in [His] presence is fullness of joy and at [His] right hand are pleasures forevermore" (Psalm 16:11).

I know that as you read this chapter, your flesh (that selfish, sinful side of your being) is likely kicking and screaming in protest, telling you how unnecessary all of this is: *You can have a close walk with God and enjoy the pleasures of this world!* or *If you lay down all these things, you'll look like a "holier-than-thou" bigot!* or *All the other Christians I know do all of these things! What's the big deal?*

But what is the Spirit of Christ whispering to your soul?

> He who has My commandments and keeps them, it is he who loves Me. And he who loves Me will be loved by My Father, and I will love him and manifest Myself to him (John 14:21).

If you want to personally experience the fullness of all that Christ is then it's time to tune out the voice of your flesh and follow the example of Paul: "But what things were gain to me, these I have counted loss for Christ. Yet indeed I also count all things loss for the excellence of the knowledge of Christ Jesus my Lord, for whom I have suffered the loss of all things, and count them as rubbish, that I may gain Christ and be found in Him...that I may know Him and the power of His resurrection, and the fellowship of His sufferings, being conformed to His death" (Philippians 3:7-10).

Yes, there will be protests when we embrace Christ's sacred decorum—both from our flesh and from the outside world. But instead of complaining about His narrow path or giving in to self-pity, let us delight in the jealous love that He has for us. Let us remember the staggering sacrifice He made on our behalf. And let us revel in the privilege of laying our all at His feet in gratitude. Let us yield to the supernatural, transforming, purifying work of Christ's Spirit as He makes us into His holy temple. Let us allow Him to change us from the selfish, cowering closet-Christians we are into the valiant, valorous, virtuous examples of set-apart femininity that God has called us to be. And let the world stand back in wonder.

> He who loves his life will lose it, and he who hates his life in this world will keep it for eternal life. If anyone serves Me, let him follow Me; and where I am, there My servant will be also. If anyone serves Me, him My Father will honor (John 12:25-26).

> Depart! Depart! Go out from there. Touch no unclean thing. Go out from the midst of her, be clean, you who bear the vessels of the LORD (Isaiah 52:11).

> Beware of reasoning about God's Word—obey it.[13]
>
> —OSWALD CHAMBERS

Sacred Mystique

femininity that changes men into princes

5

In *Authentic Beauty,* I wrote about the lost art of feminine mystique. Today it is the norm for a young woman to sensually flaunt her figure, carelessly give her heart and body to guy after guy, and scoff at the "outdated" idea of maintaining feminine mystery. On college campuses across this country, it is regarded as "healthy" for a young woman to be able to completely shut off her emotions and have mindless sex with any random guy she meets, not caring at all if he ever calls her again.

But once upon a time, feminine dignity was carefully protected. Womanly mystery was held in high esteem. And gallant men counted it a privilege to tenderly win and woo their lady-love's heart. This idea was not first born in Jane Austen novels, but in the original design of our Creator. The Song of Solomon illustrates this glorious pattern, a bride being pursued by her strong bridegroom, a woman who is fully feminine responding to a man who is fully masculine.

The sacred decorum by which Christ has called us to live must extend to our interaction with the opposite sex. "The unmarried woman cares about the things of the Lord, that she may be holy both in body and in spirit" (1 Corinthians 7:34). As set-apart young women, we are called to live in absolute purity—to be completely holy in both body and spirit. But all too many of us take our cues from the sex-goddess icons of the culture rather than from the Word of God.

Look at this picture of the adulterous woman in Proverbs. "And behold, a woman comes to meet him, dressed as a harlot and cunning of heart. She is boisterous and rebellious, her feet do not remain at home. She is now in the streets, now in the squares, and lurks by every corner. So she seizes him and kisses him and with a brazen face she (speaks) to him" (Proverbs 7:10-13 NASB).

This woman is physically aggressive toward guys, sensually dressed, always "on the prowl" for men, and uses strategic flirting and manipulation to lure guys into her seductive power. She is careless of her purity and her heart, and she looks to male approval to bring her pleasure. Sound like anyone you know? I'm guessing the answer is yes because her description fits the majority of young women in our modern culture, even most Christ-professing ones. It is considered normal for a young woman to be aggressive, flirtatious, and sensual toward guys and use her feminine allure to manipulate the opposite sex.

But what does God say about this kind of woman? Do not let your heart turn aside to her ways. Do not stray into her paths; for she has cast down many wounded, and all who were slain by her were strong men. Her house is the way to hell, descending to the chambers of death (Proverbs 7:25-27).

Wow. I'd say it's time we start taking our interactions with the opposite sex a bit more seriously! Just as we must allow God to remake our attitudes toward pop culture and worldly pursuits, we must allow Him to shape and mold our attitudes toward guys. We are called to reflect His lily-white, radiant beauty, and not a hollow sex appeal of our own making. Let's tackle three of the most common areas girls struggle with when it comes to the opposite sex.

1. Physical and Emotional Boundaries

Quite a few young women have expressed frustration to me about the "politics of guy friendships," wishing that they could simply shrug off all concern and enjoy the same closeness with their guy friends that they share with their female friends. But even though you might feel a close connection with a guy friend, it's important to stay guarded in both your thoughts and your actions toward him. It is all too easy, especially for girls, to begin giving away the kind of intimacy and affection that is meant to be saved for your future spouse. It's more than possible to enjoy close guy friendships without violating the sacredness of your future marriage relationship—but it doesn't happen by accident. It takes prayer, focus, and help from the Spirit of God.

Ask the Spirit of God to be your guide. If you submit your every thought, action, and conversation to Him, He will guide and direct you, offering caution and giving you freedom when each is needed.

Before my relationship with Eric ever began, I developed close friendships with several godly young men. Up until then, most of my interaction with the opposite sex had been flirtatious, teasing, and based on physical attraction. It was all about the challenge of getting a guy's attention or the hope of a romantic fling developing. But once I gave God the "pen" of my love story, I made a decision not to pursue guys in that way and to put a stop to the flirtatious relationships I had become so used to. I wasn't sure how to have a healthy, Christ-focused friendship with a guy. I prayed that God would show me His pattern. I found that the first step was entering into friendships with *like-minded* young men; young men who were not primarily focused on the opposite sex but on Jesus Christ. I hadn't met many young men who fell into that category, but as I prayed about it, God began to bring a small handful of them into my life. Instead of teasing, joking, and flirting when we were together, we spent time encouraging each other spiritually and discoursing about God's Word. They truly became like brothers to me, pointing me continually toward Christ and not toward themselves.

And yet, as precious as the friendships were to me, there were certain boundaries that I was always careful about. I wanted more than anything to honor my future husband in these relationships. So I asked God to direct me as I related to these young men. He showed me different ways that I could be sensitive to my future husband. I was careful about physical touch with my guy friends—a friendly, quick side hug was one thing, but I felt that front hugs invited potential stumbling. (An interjection: if you are an extremely physical, touchy-feely type of girl…you may need to make a conscious effort to hold back when you interact physically with your guy friends. Eric and I have seen far too many guys stumble because of an innocent young woman's expression of friendship through hugs and touches. Just because you "don't mean anything by it" doesn't mean that it's appropriate!)

I was also careful about how much of my intimate life I shared with my guy friends—I would talk to them about what God was teaching me but hold back on getting too personal in my sharing. I found that praying together with my guy friends was a great way to keep our focus on Christ. But even a shared time of prayer can be a form of emotional manipulation toward the opposite sex. And so I was careful not to pray about extremely deep or private issues when I was with my guy friends. None of this dampened the delight and enjoyment that I found in these guy friendships, and it gave me the assurance that my future husband was being honored and respected in the process.

In reality, a guy/girl friendship—especially one that is not headed toward marriage—is not meant to become as intimate and close as other friendships, no matter what kind of "connection" you may feel. Once God brings your future spouse into your life, your one-on-one friendships with the opposite sex will need to diminish, being replaced by "couple friendships" instead. And it is far less painful to make that transition when deep, personal, intimate bonds have not been forged.

If there is a possibility in your mind that a friendship with a member of the opposite sex might end up as something more, it is still wise to be careful until you know for sure. God is perfectly capable of nudging a relationship forward in His own time and way. But in the meantime, the best thing you can do is to live as if your heart, mind, and body still belong to someone else.

Some Guidelines for Keeping Sacred Things Sacred

God's perfect pattern for guarding sacred things in a human life is demonstrated in His amazing design for His holy temple in the Old Testament. The Hebrew temple was divided into varying degrees of sacredness. The "outer court" was sacred, but it wasn't as sacred as the "holy place." And whereas the "holy place" was sacred, it was not as sacred as the "Holy of Holies." This pattern provides a perfect guideline for knowing what to give and what to hold sacred when it comes to guys.

The Holy of Holies. This arena must never be shared or made open to the public, even to those of your most intimate circle. In the Old Testament, God separated this portion of the temple from even His most trusted workers by a thick curtain. The Holy of Holies represents the most intimate and precious areas of the human soul and body. And this supremely sacred arena of the human life is preserved for God alone and able to be shared with a spouse under the parameters of the holy marriage covenant. The Holy of Holies includes such sacred things as sexual expression, sexual touch, sexual body parts, and the deepest, most personal dimensions of the heart and mind. And it is important to note that the Song of Solomon denotes *all* forms of sexual touch as part of sexual intimacy. Giving away your physical purity is not just a matter of "crossing a line" but of sharing any part of your sexuality with someone outside of a marriage covenant.

The Holy Place. Like the Holy of Holies, this domain of the human life must not be shared with the public. However, it is accessible to more than just God and a spouse. Those of the most trustworthy character are allowed to share in this sacred arena. Family and intimate friends can be allowed into this holy sector if they first prove honorable and upright. The holy place includes such sacred things as deeply personal expression (nonsexual), deeply personal touch (nonsexual), dimensions of the heart and mind containing highly sensitive and sacred matters (hurts, vulnerabilities, fears, weaknesses, dreams, desires, longings).

The holy place should only be entered with an unrelated member of the opposite sex when you are in a serious relationship, led by God, headed toward marriage. When this holy place is entered carelessly or casually with members of the opposite sex, you can easily give away affection, attention, and emotion meant only for your future spouse and leave each other open for serious hurt and misunderstanding.

If you are married (and want to stay that way), you won't enter into a deep, intimate friendship with another guy; opening up personal, vulnerable dimensions of your heart to him instead of to your husband. So if you wouldn't enter this kind of friendship with a guy after marriage, why would you enter one *before* marriage with someone other than your spouse?

In our modern Christian culture, being "real and open" with other members of the body is considered spiritually healthy. And certainly, there is a dimension of "bearing one another's burdens" that is applauded in Scripture. But I believe that a closer look at Scripture shows that this concept has a lot more to do with *practically* helping those in need and not just sitting around airing our emotional baggage. And when we sacrifice our feminine mystique under the banner of authenticity, we violate the design of our Creator. God tells us not to exude merely a physical beauty, but to allow our beauty to flow from the "hidden person" of the heart.

> Do not let your adornment be merely outward—arranging the hair, wearing gold, or putting on fine apparel—rather let it be the hidden person of the heart (1 Peter 3:3-4).

The phrase "hidden person of the heart" refers to the secret, intimate part of who we are. But if we embrace the "hold nothing back" version of womanhood we see all around us, we have no "hidden person of the heart" left to protect; everything we think, hope, dream, fear, and feel is all out there on display for the world to see. And we end up far more like the brazen, aggressive adulteress in Proverbs 7 than the dignified and valiant woman in Proverbs 31.

Save your "private and vulnerable" conversations for like-minded sisters, parents, Christian mentors, and your prayer journal. When you guard the "hidden person of the heart" for your husband, you will experience the kind of glorious unhindered marriage intimacy God designed you to enjoy.

The Outer Court. Like the holy place, this sacred arena of the human life is open to more than just a spouse in marriage. While its stipulations are not quite as strict as the holy place, the sacred things in its domain still deserve a heightened level of guarded- ness and special protection. The outer court includes such sacred things as friendly touch, words of specific encouragement, char- acter endorsements, intercessory prayer, friendships with believ- ers, the teaching and discussing of doctrine, and communion.

These may not seem like sacred things to many, but they are, and they deserve an attitude of honor and guardedness. These

Living the set-apart life has a huge effect on how I relate to guys. Rather than seeing every eligible guy as a potential "partner," I see them as individuals to bless and protect for their future companions...whoever they may be! This enables me to be friends and keep friends with dignity and respect, without getting into playing games or trying to manipu- late circumstances. As my daddy always said, "God gives His best to those who leave the choice to Him." My parents have been happily mar- ried for over 35 years. If I marry, I plan to carry on that same legacy.

–Melody, 32

things should not be given to those who appraise not their correct value and importance (see Matthew 7:6). If you are wondering how to interact with Christian guy friends, this outer court analogy serves as a great guideline, but be sure that you are led by God's Spirit and not moved by selfish ulterior motives. Keep the honor and protection of your future spouse always in the forefront of your mind.

When Guys Won't Take the Hint

A lot of young women ask me how they should respond when a guy they aren't interested in tries to pursue a relationship. "How do I tell him to back off without hurting his feelings?" is a common question. Whether it is an ungodly guy trying to get you to lower your standards or a Christian guy enticing you to offer more of yourself than you feel is appropriate, your first concern should not be "protecting his feelings," but rather protecting the priceless treasure of your heart, emotions, and body. If you can politely send "back off" signals and he takes the hint, great. But often something more forceful is needed, such as saying clearly, "I have no interest in any kind of relationship with you," or "I don't feel it would be healthy for us to cultivate a close friendship." And if he still doesn't back down, don't hesitate to recruit the help of a "protector" such as a dad, older brother, or pastor.

Too many young women are afraid to rise up with confidence and walk firmly in their commitments. The nurturing, caring side of them doesn't like hurting people's feelings, so they end up leaving a door open for a guy when it should be nicely but firmly shut in his face.

Jesus was not primarily concerned with protecting people's feelings but with speaking the unadulterated truth. He was not mealy-mouthed where correction was concerned. He even openly called people "white washed tombs" and "a brood of vipers" when the occasion called for it (see Matthew 23).

Remember that a set-apart, Proverbs 31 woman is mighty and valiant, not wimpy and waffling. Don't hesitate to rise up in the strength of God to jealously protect the hidden person of your heart, no matter how much a guy's pride might be dented in the process. Chances are it's exactly what he needs.

2. Letting Guys Initiate

Young women frequently ask me, "Do you think guys should always be the initiators in relationships?" Usually what they really mean is, "There is this guy I am really attracted to, but nothing seems to be happening and I am getting impatient. Maybe *I* should make the first move."

While it might seem like the wise thing to do in the moment, taking the initiative with a guy violates another pattern of our Creator's design. The entire Bible is a picture of the Bridegroom with His bride. Our Bridegroom takes the first step in loving us, and we as the bride respond to His love:

> We love Him because He first loved us (1 John 4:19).

> I have loved you with an everlasting love. Therefore with loving-kindness I have drawn you (Jeremiah 31:3).

> Therefore I am now going to allure her; I will lead her into the desert and speak tenderly to her (Hosea 2:14).

The book of Song of Solomon paints a vivid illustration of a bridegroom initiating and the bride responding. He pursues her, and her womanly heart is awakened by his tender wooing.

I have yet to meet a woman who is longing for a weak, wimpy, insecure man who never takes the lead or makes decisions. One of the biggest cries of young unmarried women today is "where are all the men?" Instead of strong, confident leaders who reflect valiant "William Wallace" manhood, they see insecure followers; guys who don't seem to have a backbone or even know how to pursue a woman's heart.

But unfortunately, women aren't helping the problem. When a woman tries to take a man's role in a relationship, she robs him of his masculine strength. Sure, he may at first appear to like it when a woman pursues him. After all, it saves him the insecurity of sticking his neck out or having to go to the effort of carefully winning her heart. He may be temporarily flattered by her aggression toward him, but in the end, he will lose respect for both her and his own masculinity. Instead of becoming her protector and leader, he will become lazy and lackluster, expecting her to do all the work in the relationship.

On the flip side, if a woman allows a man to rise to the challenge of pursuing her, wooing her, and winning her heart over time, instead of thrusting it upon him too readily, his masculine strength will be tested and strengthened. Once he has pursued and won his prize according to God's perfect pattern, he is far less likely to take her for granted. Rather, he will become the heroic protector he was created to be— laying down his life to preserve and nurture the heart of the princess whom he worked so hard to win.

A strong, confident, heroic man who rises to the challenge of winning a woman's heart, then carefully protects and preserves his hard-won prize…this is the ultimate romantic desire of nearly every woman I have ever talked to. And yet, ironically, all too many women are actually robbing men of these very qualities, simply by their own impatience. They are in such a hurry to snag a man that they don't wait for him to initiate—they take the lead, become the pursuer instead of the pursued, and in so doing, strip their man of all the strong masculine qualities they so desire him to have.

I struggled with this problem greatly during my single years. Growing up, my parents exhorted me over and over again that men were more attracted to women who allowed the guy to take the lead—but to me it seemed that the super-aggressive girls were the ones to get all the male attention. I wondered, *If I wait for a guy to pursue me, how can I be sure that anyone ever will? Isn't this idea of men needing to be the initiator an outdated concept anyway?*

Even in my blossoming friendship with Eric, this question plagued me. As our friendship progressed, it seemed obvious that something more was beginning to develop between us—and yet, he did not initiate a conversation about it. So I waited. I prayed. I came close so many times to initiating a conversation about where the friendship was going. But God's Spirit continued to hold me back.

Finally when the time was right, Eric took the lead. And one of the first things that he said to me was how much it meant to him that I had allowed him to be the one to initiate a conversation about our relationship. "You respected my position as a man," he told me, "and not many girls today would do that."

Even when Eric expressed feelings for me that went beyond friendship, I felt God caution me not to offer my heart to him too readily or quickly. With His gentle and faithful direction, I opened my heart to Eric slowly, gradually, as he proved by his honor, respect, and integrity that he was worthy of such a gift. He did not respond to my hesitation with impatience or disgust. Rather, he rose to the challenge and seemed to respect me all the more as I protected and guarded my feminine mystique. And as a result, I felt like a princess being pursued by a gallant prince.

That's when I realized that we can only experience the absolute beauty, sacredness, and perfection of God's perfect pattern for romance when we fulfill the masculine and feminine roles He created for us.

One of the biggest complaints I hear from married women is that the husband doesn't take a leadership position in the marriage—which often leads to a lot of fruitless nagging and criticizing on the wife's part. Quite often, this problem in these marriages emerged long before the wedding day—at the very beginning of the relationship. The woman took the lead, became the initiator, and inadvertently stepped into the role that God designed the man to hold. Then the unhealthy pattern was carried into the marriage relationship, setting the stage for frustration and disillusionment.

Girls, if you desire your future husband to be a strong, confident leader in the relationship, then let the relationship begin according to God's pattern. Allow the man to be the initiator, the leader, and the pursuer.

One of my good friends, Natalie, had a close guy friend, Jason, whom she respected and admired very much. They seemed to share a connection that went beyond mere friendship, and Natalie was unable to shake the strong feeling that this man could be God's intended future husband for her. But years went by, and still Jason did not initiate anything more than friendship. At times he seemed interested in something more, but he never made any move in that direction.

"Why shouldn't I just initiate a conversation with him about how I feel?" she wondered many times. "What's so wrong with just being open and honest about what I think God might be doing between us?" But after much prayer, she decided that she would leave it in God's hands. "If God wants us to be together, He is perfectly capable of prompting Jason to take the lead," she decided.

Finally, after Natalie had all but given up on the hope of a relationship ever happening, Jason approached her. He told her that he felt God leading him to pursue a romantic relationship with her, and he expressed his gratitude that she had waited patiently for him to take the lead. He began to pursue her heart, and when he had fully won it, he cherished it with everything in him. It became a beautiful, sacred, God-glorifying relationship. And it started with true femininity allowing true masculinity to shine.

"If I had rushed ahead with my own agenda," she told me later, "I would have missed out on the greatest gift that God had for me. I allowed Jason to be the man in our relationship. And now, he treats me like a princess—he stands up for me, protects me, and honors me in every way. I am so glad I followed God's pattern!"

God's ways can often seem old-fashioned in our modern mode of thinking. But His pattern never becomes outdated and His ways never go out of style. God's pattern restores the long lost art of masculine nobility and feminine dignity—returning us to the days of gallant lords and fair maidens. Following God's design is what sets the stage for those seemingly impossible dreams to actually come true. If finding our deepest romantic longings fulfilled is what comes of following God's design, then I think we need more of His amazing "old-fashioned" ways!

3. Flirting

In our book *Meet Mr. Smith*, I shared my perspective on flirting:

In modern relationships, flirting seems about as innocent and harmless as window shopping at the mall. "What's the harm of browsing, as long as you don't actually buy anything?" a young man named Chris jokingly asked us during a discussion on the topic.

Even young people who have chosen God's pattern for relationships and are seeking to live a set-apart life for their future spouse often shrug off flirting as a natural part of any male/female interaction. But take a closer look at what flirting really is, and it becomes clear that some important principles in God's pattern are violated by doing it.

Flirting is, in essence, drawing another person's attention toward you. It is using your feminine power to entice another person to notice, admire, and be attracted to you. It is putting your personality, body, humor, and wit on display—playing a game in which you score more points the more positive attention you receive from the other person.

Flirting, at its core, is based in selfishness.

If Eric flirted with other women, I would be hurt, jealous, and angry. If I flirted with other men, he would feel outraged and betrayed. We are in a covenant marriage relationship and have pledged to have eyes only for each other. I belong to Eric—mind, body, and heart. And he belongs to me. We honor each other by keeping our attentions sacred—reserved for our spouse alone. Most would agree that this is the way it should be.

If then, as a married person you would not dishonor or hurt your spouse by flirting with anyone else, why would you hurt your future spouse now by flirting with others before marriage? As you interact with guys, ask yourself this question: If your future spouse was standing beside you, seeing you interact with the opposite sex, how would he feel? Once you ask that question and answer honestly, flirting no longer becomes a harmless, innocent activity.[1]

The goal in any God-centered relationship should be to continually point the other person toward Christ, not continually draw attention toward you. In my friendship with Eric, my dad made an important observation. "The reason I know that your friendship with my daughter is from God," he told Eric, "is because ever since you have been in her life, she has grown *closer* to Him." When I spent time with Eric, he did not try to get me to notice, admire, and respect him. Rather, his goal was to encourage me in my relationship with Christ and help me draw closer to God through his example. After spending time around Eric, I didn't come home wanting to sit around and daydream about *him,* rather I came home wanting to focus even more on *Jesus Christ.* This pattern laid the foundation for a marriage relationship in which both of us continually point the other toward Christ—and as a result, we naturally draw closer to each other while keeping Christ in His rightful position as the focus and center of our relationship.

It's impossible to point someone to Jesus Christ through flirting. You can lay the foundation even now for a Christ-focused relationship by taking flirting out of your lifestyle. If you make it your goal to draw guys' attention toward Christ rather than toward you, you'll be amazed at how natural it will be to build a truly Christ-centered love story when the time comes.

If you aren't sure where the line is between friendliness and flirting, ask God's Spirit to direct you as you interact with guys. And when in doubt, it's best to err on the side of caution, not presumption. If your goal is to point guys toward Christ and guard your feminine mystique for your future husband, He will be faithful to lead you in the specifics of how this plays out in daily life.

And remember that God is perfectly capable of bringing a relationship to you in His perfect time and way, without your using flirtatious feminine powers to manipulate the situation. If you allow Him to hold the pen and write your story, you'll be astounded at His perfect faithfulness.

Sacred Cultivation

unearthing femininity's valiant strength

6

> One of these days some simple soul will pick up the Book of God, read it and believe it.[1]
>
> —LEONARD RAVENHILL

Last year I read the autobiography of Hudson Taylor—the heroic missionary to China whom our son is named after. At the age of 17, Hudson was living a mediocre Christian life and continually being pulled toward sin. He could feel the call of God upon his soul, but he seemed unable to respond the way he desired to. Many nights were spent in despair, wondering if he would ever find real victory. Finally, he decided to pray. He went into his room, locked his door, fell upon his knees, and cried out to God from the depths of his being.

And the King of the universe heard him. He answered in a more powerful way than Hudson could ever have imagined. A few days later he wrote these words to his sister.

> Bless the Lord, O my soul! And all that is within me shout His praise! Glory to God, my dear Amelia. Christ has said, "seek and ye shall find," and praise His name, He has revealed Himself

to me in an overflowing manner. He has cleansed me from all
sin, from all my idols. He has given me a new heart. Glory,
glory, glory to His ever blessed Name! I cannot write for joy.[2]

The freedom and triumph that God gave Hudson Taylor was not
just a fleeting "mountaintop experience." Rather, he was completely
and radically set free—never to look back. The rest of Hudson's life
was a glorious display of a supernaturally enabled existence. He sailed
to a godless, hostile land, led countless thousands into the kingdom
of God, and became the sole inspiration for an entire generation of
Christians to "go into all the world and make disciples of all nations."
Though he lived 200 years ago, his legacy is still cherished and his
example still followed by millions.

O magnify the LORD with me, and let us exalt his name together.
I sought the LORD, and he heard me, and delivered me from all
my fears. They looked unto him and were lightened, and their
faces were not ashamed (Psalm 34:3-5 KJV).

Stories like Hudson's are extremely unusual in today's world. Most
modern Christians I have talked to have the *opposite* experience when
it comes to seeking God. Instead of radically answered prayer, they
get only silence from heaven. Instead of victory and triumph in their
daily life, they get only defeat and discouragement. And instead of
a supernaturally enabled life that inspires millions, they struggle to
even inspire their own friends and family members. I've even heard
Christians say that men like Hudson Taylor only come along once or
twice in every generation—and that the rest of us shouldn't expect
anything so grand or glorious in our walk with God.

But once upon a time, the Christian life meant something different
than a blasé daily struggle. In the "olden days," stories like Hudson
Taylor's weren't quite so rare. Following Christ actually meant exceeding joy, peace that passes all understanding, and power to trounce upon
our enemies. Just look at the lyrics of some of the old hymns:

Pardon for sin and a peace that endureth—
Thine own dear presence to cheer and to guide;
Strength for today and bright hope for tomorrow,
Blessings all mine with ten thousand beside.
Great is Thy faithfulness, Lord, unto me![3]

"Great Is Thy Faithfulness," words by Thomas Chrisholm, 1923

He speaks, and the sound of His voice
Is so sweet the birds hush their singing,
And the melody that He gave to me
Within my heart is ringing.
And He walks with me, and He talks with me,
And He tells me I am His own;
And the joy we share as we tarry there,
None other has ever known.

"In the Garden," words and music by C. Austin Miles, 1912

Blessed assurance, Jesus is mine!
O what a foretaste of glory divine!
Heir of salvation, purchase of God,
Born of His Spirit, washed in His blood.
Perfect submission, all is at rest.
I in my Savior am happy and blessed,
Watching and waiting, looking above,
Filled with His goodness, lost in His love.
This is my story, this is my song,
Praising my Savior all the day long.

"Blessed Assurance," words by Fanny Crosby, 1873

A mighty fortress is our God; a bulwark never failing;
Our helper He, amid the flood of mortal ills prevailing.
And though this world, with devils filled,
    should threaten to undo us,
We will not fear, for God hath willed
    His truth to triumph through us.

"A MIGHTY FORTRESS IS OUR GOD," WORDS AND MUSIC BY
MARTIN LUTHER, 1529

But we don't sing songs like these anymore because their messages just don't ring true in our lives. Most of us would feel like hypocrites (or idiots) if we actually stood up in church with huge smiles on our faces and proclaimed the words of the old hymn: "Jesus! Jesus! Sweetest name I know! Fills my every longing, keeps me singing as I go!"

A church in our local area is fond of using songs by Creed and U2 in their worship service because "our people can relate so much better to the lyrics." One of their favorites is the U2 hit "I Still Haven't Found What I'm Looking For." Those words seem to sum up what nearly every modern Christian feels in regard to his or her walk with God. It's no wonder that particular church is one of the largest in the state.

A long-time missionary recently told me, "We sell people a bill of goods when we tell them that Jesus is the answer to all their problems. The reality is that they are still going to have lots of struggles, even after they come to Christ, so we shouldn't paint Christianity to be some amazing experience."

Our Christian bookstores are loaded with books like *Disappointment with God, When God Doesn't Make Sense,* and *Deserted by God?.* Modern Christian leaders spend an inordinate amount of time trying to help us "cope" with the disappointment, disillusionment, and depression that seems to go hand in glove with following Christ these days.

Not long ago I stumbled across a Christian book for women called *Waking Up from the Dream of a Lifetime: Real Life Stuff for Women on Disappointment.* The publisher's description is as follows:

> You once dreamed of a life of Prince Charmings and fairy-tale endings. But now that you've grown up and arrived at womanhood, those dreams seem so far out of reach. Your husband isn't quite the guy you thought you married, your kids face challenges you never dreamed of, you have to work a lot more than you expected just to make ends meet, your spiritual life is a joke, and even the bedroom wallpaper you saved up for just looks wrong. How in the world can you cope with constant disappointment at every level of life? If your life feels far off the mark, you can overcome the disappointment with this stimulating new discussion guide. It brings together literary and cultural insights, conversation starters, and key passages from *The Message.* And it will give you fresh, realistic hope and purpose for the days ahead.[4]

I don't know about you, but I feel depressed after the first few sentences. Why would we even want to follow Christ if *that* dismal picture is what we have to look forward to? For that matter, why would we even get out of bed in the morning?

As young women, do we need a dose of "realistic" hope for the days ahead as this book prescribes? Or do we need to understand the *spectacular, extraordinary, mind-boggling* hope that Christ brings? As we discussed in the last chapter, Jesus said, "I have come that they may have life, and that they may have it more abundantly" (John 10:10). *Abundantly* means beyond measure, over and above all that we could ask or think. Not day to day surviving, but day to day *thriving.* As Paul says, "Now to Him who is able to do exceedingly abundantly above all that we ask or think, according to the power that works in us, to

Him be glory in the church by Christ Jesus to all generations, forever and ever" (Ephesians 3:20).

So why are our expectations of Him so dismally low? Why does the God of the Bible not seem to be the same as the God of our own experience?

There are a slew of popular Christian books and messages that have recently emerged onto the scene with the intent of shedding light upon that very question. Some say it is because we have overstretched the promises of the Bible and expected too much of God. Others say we have leaned too heavily upon the Bible as the absolute, literal truth; and that Scripture is merely a collection of human-concocted stories that should be loosely interpreted through the lens of our changing culture. (For more specifics on these messages, see Eric's book, *The Bravehearted Gospel.*)

But I am going to offer a different answer to the question that burns upon our generation's disillusioned heart. I believe with every ounce of conviction I possess that the Bible means exactly what it says, and that we cannot even comprehend how enormous our God is or how much He desires to do in and through our lives. As it says in 1 Corinthians 2:9, "Eye has not seen, nor ear heard, nor have entered into the heart of man the things that God has prepared for those who love Him."

Our problem is not that we expect too much of God, but that we expect *far too little* of Him. Just look at this brief sampling of the many great and precious promises of our Lord.

He will supernaturally protect us from harm.

> You shall not be afraid of the terror by night, nor of the arrow that flies by day, nor of the pestilence that walks in darkness, nor of the destruction that lays waste at noonday. A thousand may fall at your side, and ten thousand at your right hand; but it shall not come near you. Only with your eyes shall you look and see the reward of the wicked. Because you have made the LORD, who

is my refuge, even the Most High, your dwelling place, no evil shall befall you, nor shall any plague come near your dwelling, for He shall give His angels charge over you, to keep you in all your ways. In their hands they shall bear you up, lest you dash your foot against a stone (Psalm 91:5-12).

He will save, heal, and rescue us from destruction and fill us with good things.

Bless the LORD, O my soul; and all that is within me, bless His holy name! Bless the LORD, O my soul, and forget not all His benefits. Who forgives all your iniquities? Who heals all your diseases? Who redeems your life from destruction? Who crowns you with lovingkindness and tender mercies? Who satisfies your mouth with good things so that your youth is renewed like the eagle's? (Psalm 103:1-4).

He will not withhold any good thing from us.

For the LORD God is a sun and shield; the LORD will give grace and glory. No good thing will He withhold from those who walk uprightly. O LORD of hosts, blessed is the man who trusts in You! (Psalm 84:11-12).

He will give us supernatural strength and power.

He gives power to the weak, and to those who have no might He increases strength. Even the youths shall faint and be weary, and the young men shall utterly fall, but those who wait on the LORD shall renew their strength. They shall mount up with wings like eagles. They shall run and not be weary. They shall walk and not faint (Isaiah 40:29-31).

He will keep us in perfect peace as we look to Him.

You will keep him in perfect peace whose mind is stayed on You because he trusts in You (Isaiah 26:3).

He will do even beyond what we ask or think.

Now to Him who is able to do exceedingly abundantly above all that we ask or think, according to the power that works in us, to Him be glory in the church by Christ Jesus to all generations, forever and ever (Ephesians 3:20-21).

He will give us victory over sin.

For the law of the Spirit of life in Christ Jesus hath made me free from the law of sin and death. For what the law could not do, in that it was weak through the flesh, God sending his own Son in the likeness of sinful flesh, and for sin, condemned sin in the flesh: that the righteousness of the law might be fulfilled in us, who walk not after the flesh, but after the Spirit. For they that are after the flesh do mind the things of the flesh; but they that are after the Spirit the things of the Spirit. For to be carnally minded is death; but to be spiritually minded is life and peace (Romans 8:2-6 KJV).

He will give us power over the enemy.

Resist the devil and he will flee from you (James 4:7).

He will stand against all who stand against us.

"No weapon formed against you shall prosper, and every tongue which rises against you in judgment, you shall condemn.

This is the heritage of the servants of the LORD and their righteousness is from Me," says the LORD (Isaiah 54:17).

There are only two ways to respond to God's extreme and abundant promises. We can explain them away, as many theologians and
modern writers have done, and live as if they do not apply to our daily
moment-by-moment life. Or we can actually believe them and build
our life around them.

We have adopted the convenient theory that the Bible is a Book
to be explained, whereas first and foremost it is a Book to be
believed (and after that obeyed).[5]

—LEONARD RAVENHILL

In our book *When God Writes Your Life Story,* Eric and I talk about
the *endless frontier* of God's kingdom. Instead of taking one or two
steps forward with Christ and then stopping and pitching our tent, we
are called to be spiritual pioneers, continually exploring the fathomless
depths of the fullness of Christ. No matter what we know about Jesus
now, there is always more to be discovered and experienced. In fact,
even eternity won't be long enough to fully grasp His insurmountable
glory and brilliance. T. Austin Sparks said it well, "The mark of a life
governed by the Holy Spirit is that such a life is continually and ever
more and more occupied with Christ, that Christ is becoming greater
and greater as time goes on. Oh the depths, the fullness of Christ! If
we live as long as ever man lived, we shall still be only on the fringe of
this vast fullness that Christ is."[6]

Eric and I have personally experienced a taste of God's "endless
frontier" in many areas of our lives. In our love story, instead of building our relationship the same way the rest of the world did (with a few
Christian morals tagged on), we allowed God to script each detail of
our romance. The result was a love story more fulfilling and beautiful
than anything we could have imagined or hoped for.

In seeking victory over sin, instead of saying, "this will always defeat me," we have allowed the conquering grace of Christ to triumph in and through us and set us free from sin's controlling vise. (Yes, we are still human, prone to stumble and compromise, but by God's grace, we have not allowed habitual sin to rule our lives.)

But even with the many blessings and victories God has given us, this past year has catapulted us even further into His amazing, fathomless frontier. I'd like to give you a little peek into our journey.

We have been in full-time ministry for nearly 12 years. And I wish I could say that it has always been triumphant and full of victory. But the truth is that, though we enjoyed blessings in so many areas of our lives, there were many negative experiences associated with our service in God's kingdom. It seemed that every time we tried to step out and fulfill the call of God upon our lives, a million roadblocks would stand in our way. We grew to accept things like financial crisis, relational betrayal and backstabbing, exhaustion, stress, and health problems as normal.

We saw countless promises in the Bible about the bountiful blessings of God, but we assumed that this incredible abundance and supernatural provision should not be expected in *every* area of life. After all, there were plenty of Scriptures about God disciplining His children and taking them through trials. So we figured that all of the difficulty, stress, and chaos in our lives were things He was allowing in order to teach us patience and dependence.

And then the attacks on our life began to intensify. We lost our second child to a miscarriage. We were hit with bizarre financial catastrophes. (For example, our car engine died just days after the warranty expired, leaving us with thousands of dollars in repairs—and this happened with two cars, one right after the other!) Ministry became stressful and difficult. And every time we tried to take a step forward into something God was calling us to, one of us would inevitably be hit with some kind of debilitating sickness.

I read that the Proverbs 31 woman "smiled at the days to come," but after everything we'd been through, I found myself constantly *worrying* about the days to come. What else was God going to take me through? How much of this did He think I could handle?

I found myself subconsciously pulling away from an intimate relationship with God. For intimacy to flourish, there must be implicit trust. And I found that I no longer really trusted Him with all of my heart. I had always believed Him to be a Father who gave "good and perfect gifts" to His children, but that didn't really seem true anymore. His Word exhorted me to have faith in His goodness and mercy, but how could I have faith when it seemed He had let me down so many times? How could I trust Him as a loving Father when He'd become a stern, reprimanding authority figure, always sending another miserable trial my way to keep my spirit broken? Scripture beckoned me to "be anxious for nothing." But could I banish anxiety when I was constantly bracing for the next blow?

I spent several weeks desperately crying out to God for answers. I knew that something was building a wall between Him and me, and with all my heart I longed for it to be removed. *Lord,* I prayed, *show me what is standing in the way of my ability to walk in the victory, strength, joy, and peace You intended for my life.*

He answered that cry of my heart—more faithfully and more fully than I ever could have imagined. Gently and lovingly, He opened my eyes to see His face more clearly and understand His nature as never before. And in the process, He armed me with a measure of strength and triumph I never knew He intended me to have.

In the past two years, I have truly tasted of the "old time victory" in a greater measure than ever before. Now when I sing the ancient hymns of praise or read the joyful Psalms, I can *sincerely* echo the happy words from the depths of my being. I can genuinely shout from the rooftops, "Magnify the LORD with me! I sought the LORD and He answered me, and delivered me from all my fears" (Psalm 34:3-4 NASB).

If you have ever struggled with trusting God or wondered why He seems to always fail and disappoint you, this next section can change your life. As you read it, instead of falling for the "God really isn't that impressive" messages of today, ask God to reveal Himself to you as the merciful, tender, faithful, and *perfect* Father He is. And when He does, you will truly be able to smile at the days to come, without fear, for the rest of your life.

Pain—Friend or Foe?

Kelly is a radiant young woman who is radically surrendered to Christ. In a recent email to me she wrote, "What great joy I am finding in the yielded, set-apart life! What a privilege to commune and talk with my Lord Jesus; depending upon Him for even the slightest need."

> It is Christ alone who equips me with the passion and energy I need to be an effective teacher. He gives me the joy, and I mean JOY, each day so that I wake up ready to take on the day. In fact, He fills me with joy to such an extent that the janitor at my school has said it's unnatural for someone to be as cheerful as I am. When he asked me about it, I gladly said, "It's Jesus, not me!"
>
> —Jolene, 26

Her words sum up the secret to overcoming all fear, anxiety, and depression...depending upon our faithful Lord for even the *slightest* need. The reason that so many of us are weighed down by unnecessary burdens is because we don't take them to Jesus. We don't understand that He truly holds the answer to every problem we could ever face. The help He gives is not merely spiritual, but practical. Jesus Christ does not just want to be our Savior, He wants to be our all in all—our *everything.* Here is a quick glimpse at what Scripture says He is to us.

He is my Portion (Psalm 73:26), my Maker, my Husband (Isaiah 54:5), my Well-beloved (Song of Solomon 1:13), my Savior (2 Peter 3:18), my Hope (1 Timothy 1:1), my Brother (Mark 3:35), my Helper (Hebrews 13:6), my Physician (Jeremiah 8:22), my Healer (Luke 9:11), my Refiner (Malachi 3:3), my Purifier (Malachi 3:3), my Lord, Master (John 13:13), my Servant (Luke 12:37), my Example (John 13:15), my Teacher (John 3:2), my Shepherd (Psalm 23:1), my Keeper (John 17:12), my

Feeder (Ezekiel 34:23), my Leader (Isaiah 40:11), my Restorer (Psalm 23:3), my Resting-place (Jeremiah 50:6), my Meat (John 6:55), my Drink (John 6:55), my Passover (1 Corinthians 5:7), my Peace (Ephesians 2:14), my Wisdom (1 Corinthians 1:30), my Righteousness (1 Corinthians 1:30), my Sanctification (1 Corinthians 1:30), my Redemption (1 Corinthians 1:30), and my All in All (Colossians 3:11).

But most of us don't allow Him to be all of those things to us. In fact, many of us see Christ as the *opposite* of a gentle, loving, merciful Shepherd who is faithful to meet our every need.

A young woman named Kelsie recently told me, "I feel like I'm getting body-slammed by God, and now I am beaten-down and covered with bruises." Kelsie might be getting body-slammed, but it isn't God's doing. Our King doesn't show violence toward His children or leave them full of bruises. He is goodness and love personified. If we are being spiritually body-slammed, we can be assured that it is *not* coming from the Prince of Peace, but from the prince of darkness. All too often, when the enemy attacks us with darkness and confusion, we assume that our Lord is causing or allowing it. But in reality we are attributing something to God that is completely contrary to His nature.

If anyone fiercely assails you it will not be from Me (Isaiah 54:15 NASB).

As I prayed about the fierce attacks upon my life, God gently opened my eyes to realize that the hits were not coming from Him—they were coming from the enemy of my soul. God did not want me to resign myself to accepting these attacks. Rather, He wanted me to call upon His name and allow Him to come to my rescue. James 4:7 says, "Resist the devil and he will flee from you." I hadn't been resisting the enemy's blows because I had assumed they were coming from God—or at least being *allowed* by God for the purpose of discipline. And yet, when I really thought about it, I had to admit that the result in my spiritual life wasn't the life-giving victory that God's loving discipline brings. Rather, it was the hopeless despair and discouragement that the enemy brings. I had always thought the most God-pleasing thing I could do when bad things happened was to simply accept them and move on. But God was showing me that when the enemy attacked, He didn't want me to accept it. He wanted me to stand up and *fight* by the power of His Spirit.

To become the valiant set-apart Proverbs 31 woman we are called to be, we cannot just roll over and play dead when the enemy attacks us. We must stand firm and resist (in the mighty power of Christ's name) and not allow Satan to hinder God's purposes for our lives. As it says in Ephesians, "Be strong in the Lord and in the power of His might. Put on the whole armor of God, that you may be able to stand against the wiles of the devil" (Ephesians 6:10-11).

But if we are going to effectively resist the enemy's attacks, we must learn to recognize them. We have to stop blaming God for the enemy's devices against us. Yes, God disciplines us and refines us, but not in harsh, cruel ways. God's ways bring light, not darkness, and life, not death. Let's look at the stark difference between the way God works and the way Satan works.

Light Versus Darkness

First Peter 2:9 says that God has called us out of darkness into His marvelous light. Think about the qualities of light: clear, not confused, not blurry, but bright, cheerful, and hopeful. The opposite of light is darkness. Satan is the prince of darkness, meaning he is the prince of all things fearful, confused, indistinct, dim, and forbidding. *Anything of confusion, fear, or darkness is not from God.*

Life Versus Death

John 10:10 says that Christ came to give abundant life, not death. The qualities of abundant life are happiness, health, wholeness, strength, purity, spiritual success, and multiplication of blessing. The characteristics of death are disease, sickness, blindness, deafness, muteness, lameness, disorder, feebleness, erosion of strength, erosion of blessing, and erosion of resources. *Anything that breeds these qualities of death in our lives is not from God.*

Father of Lights Versus Father of Lies

James 1:17 says that God is the Father of lights in whom is no shadow of turning. In Scripture the Father of lights is defined as the giver of good and perfect gifts, who is merciful, long-suffering, gentle, quick to forgive, strong to protect, able and eager to rescue us, and a tender deliverer from all that would ensnare us. The enemy, on the other hand, is the father of lies—a snuffer of life and hope, a condemner, a whisperer of fault, a noisome critic of the soul, a doubter of God's ability, a persecutor of the spirit, an advocate for the flesh, a constant diminisher of God's fatherly nature. *Anything that causes us to lose hope or diminishes our confidence in God is not from our Lord.*

Discipline Versus Abuse

Hebrews 12:5-7 compares godly discipline to the discipline of a loving, devoted father. This kind of discipline is expressed tenderly, in love. It is minimized to the level of need, brings about greater strength and health, and it is always presented with the hope of reconciliation and the fostering of even deeper intimacy with Him. The enemy works only in the arena of abuse. He is cruel, angry, harsh, extreme, and breathes threats of abandonment and forsaking. Satan's abuse injures, makes sick, breaks the spirit, and hinders and disrupts intimacy. *Anything of an abusive nature that comes against us is not from God.*

Bridegroom Versus Harsh Husband

Christ is called our loving Bridegroom all throughout Scripture. The loving Bridegroom is a patient listener, affectionate, an advocate and rescuer, willing to give up His life to save, and quick to respond to the needs of His bride. Words of love and kindness are constantly on His tongue, and prayers are continually ebbing forth for the benefit of His beloved. The enemy's ways are like that of a harsh husband; one who is impatient, cold, and haughty, never pleased, distant, demanding, controlling, verbally and physically abusive, selfish, and feigning tenderness only to get what he wants. *Anything of the nature of a harsh husband that comes against us is not from God.*

Shepherd Versus Roaring Lion

John 10:11-15 defines Christ as a good shepherd who lays down His life for His sheep. As our shepherd He is deeply interested and concerned in even the smallest matter, watchful, and constantly alert to the needs of His own. He never tires. He never sleeps. He is always looking upon His lambs with an affectionate gaze, ready to fight and defeat any fiend who would dare attack those under His care. Satan is defined as a roaring lion in First Peter 5:8. A roaring lion is the opposite of a good shepherd. He looks to control through fear instead of love. He rules through intimidation, not respect. He makes demands and threatens severe punishments if not obeyed. He makes the soul anxious and tense (rather than the absolute peace that is promised by the Shepherd in Psalm 23). The enemy roars loudly about his power and constantly yells, "Beware! The enemy is more powerful than you!" *Anything of the "roaring lion" nature that comes against us is not from God.*

If you are ever uncertain about which challenges you should resist and which you should accept, the above list can serve as a guide. We are to gladly embrace any hardship that truly comes from God, while firmly resisting any difficulty that comes from the enemy. The pain that God brings curbs our flesh and strengthens the life of His Spirit within us; things like giving up worldly popularity and applause, leaving a relationship that is drawing us away from our King, or reaching out to people who are difficult to love. These might be painful steps to take—but they bring life, hope, victory, and peace rather than darkness, despair, and defeat. It's like athletic training—there is a "pain" associated with getting in shape, but it is a healthy, fruitful, productive pain that produces *positive* results.

There might be times when God does allow us to experience "enemy pain," such as being thrown into a concentration camp or being tortured for our faith. God does not cause "concentration camp pain" or take delight in it, but He offers us the supreme privilege of suffering for His name's sake. Paul says,

> "Therefore I am well content with weaknesses, with insults, with distresses, with persecutions, with difficulties, for Christ's sake; for when I am weak, then I am strong" (2 Corinthians 12:10 NASB).

We are to glory in suffering when it is *for Christ's sake* and brings honor to His name, like Vibia Perpetua who willingly allowed her body to be ravaged by wild beasts in the arena. But we are not to glory in suffering that actually hinders the work of Christ in our hearts and thwarts His purposes for our lives. Most young women I know are stymied and cannot move forward with Christ because of the constant badgering of the enemy. Whether it be fear, anxiety, depression, guilt, confusion, insecurity, family problems, health problems, financial problems, or spiritual defeat, the enemy has gone out of his way to keep us completely preoccupied with our problems and unable to live the glorious, radiant set-apart life God has called us to live. We spend most of our time stumbling through the darkness instead of being the light of the world.

It's time for the pattern to shift. Christ said, "Behold, I give you the authority to trample on serpents and scorpions, and over all the power of the enemy, and nothing shall by any means hurt you" (Luke 10:19). So why are we living like helpless victims to Satan's schemes?

Catherine Booth (the mother of the Salvation Army) once wrote these words to her spiritually struggling daughter, "Do not give way to lowness while you are young. Rise up on the strength of God and resolve to conquer!"[7]

If the glorious promises of God are more theoretical than actual facts in our lives, we should never just accept them as reality. Rather we should rise up on the strength of God and resolve to conquer all that stands in the way of the abundant, thriving, victorious, set-apart lives He has called us to live.

Fortification
The Impervious Christian Life

When Gladys Aylward was on her way to China to fulfill the call of God on her life, the enemy must have known how powerful her ministry would be because he tried to thwart her before she even arrived. In Russia, she was detained by corrupt government officials. As she sat in a hotel room, thinking about a way to escape, an officer tried to force his way in. Boldly she told him, "You are not coming in here."

"Why not?" he smirked.

"Because this is my bedroom."

"I am the master, I can do with you what I wish!"

"Oh no, you cannot. You may not believe in God, but He is here. Touch me and see. Between you and me God has put a barrier. Go!" The man stared at Gladys, shivered, and without another word, turned and left.[8]

Imagine having that much confidence in the protection that God promises His children! Not just *hoping* God will come through for you, but *knowing* He will. Not cowering in fear when the enemy tries to attack, but rising up in the strength of God and trampling him under our feet.

Heroic Christians throughout the centuries have exuded this very confidence:

Should all the hosts of death and powers of hell unknown put their most dreadful forms of rage or malice on, I shall be safe, for Christ displays superior power and guardian grace.

−ISAAC WATTS

I fear not the tyranny of man, neither yet what the devil can invent against me.

−JOHN KNOX

The only saving faith is that which casts itself on God for life or death.

−MARTIN LUTHER

When Satan heard the ninety-first Psalm, did the fourth verse baffle him? "With His feathers He shall create a fence for thee." So covered, and so fenced, what can Satan's malice accomplish against us? Nothing, nothing at all.[9]

−AMY CARMICHAEL

Despite the popular notion today that it is more spiritual to remain weak, struggling, and vulnerable, God desires to build us into valiant, valorous, fortified warriors who fear none but Him alone and are vulnerable to none but Him alone. As I mentioned previously, the chief word that characterizes the Proverbs 31 woman is *strength*. And all throughout the New Testament, we are constantly exhorted to be *strong* in the Lord and in the power of His might.

> Satan fools and feigns, blows and bluffs, and we so often take
> his threats to heart and forget the "exceeding greatness of God's
> power to us."[10]
>
> —LEONARD RAVENHILL

Christ has already conquered the enemy of our souls. The only thing Satan can do is put on a magic show; using smoke and mirrors to trick us into taking him seriously and letting him have his way in our lives. But if we stand firmly in the power that Christ has given us, "no weapon formed against us can prosper" (see Isaiah 54:17).

How do we gain that kind of unshakable confidence? We must become *fortified* Christians. A fortified Christian woman has an impenetrable barrier between her and the enemy. She has put on the full armor of God and is able to resist the devil, no matter what fiery dart he tries to throw at her.

The book of Nehemiah paints a vivid illustration of the fortification process that produces a Gladys Aylward–like strength. At the beginning of the story, Nehemiah is in mourning, because the wall around the city of Jerusalem has been destroyed, leaving the children of Israel utterly defenseless against enemy attacks: "The survivors who are left from the captivity in the province are there in great distress and reproach. The wall of Jerusalem is also broken down, and its gates are burned with fire" (Nehemiah 1:3).

What a perfect description of our spiritual lives! Most of us live in a state of distress, hounded on all sides by the enemy, and our defeated lives are a reproach to the name of Christ. There are no protective walls around us, and we are defenseless against Satan's attacks. We go around nursing anger toward God for allowing bad things to happen to us, all the while forgetting that we have an enemy who is hell-bent on destroying us. And he will succeed as long as we leave our battle weapons untouched on the ground and the walls around our cities in shambles.

But the good news is that God is ready and willing to help us build walls of fortification around our lives and to give us every weapon needed to not just defend ourselves against Satan's schemes, but to storm the very gates of hell…and win. In Hebrews, Paul describes the heroism of God's faithful servants throughout the ages. "Who through faith subdued kingdoms, worked righteousness, obtained promises, stopped the mouths of lions, quenched the violence of fire, escaped the edge of the sword, out of weakness were made strong, became valiant in battle, turned to flight the armies of the aliens" (Hebrews 11:33-34).

Notice that all of these men and women "out of weakness were made strong." They went from being weak and frail to being so strong in God's power that they could stop the mouths of lions and put armies to flight. It's that *very same strength* that God desires to work in each one of us. You may feel weak, frail, and vulnerable, but He is ready to make you stronger than you ever thought possible. Remember the valiance of David? He was only a lowly shepherd boy—the very least of all his brothers. But God gave him such mighty valor that he killed lions and bears with his bare hands, slew a fierce giant with only a slingshot, and wiped out and destroyed the most powerful armies in the world. What God did for David, He wants to do for you and me.

So, if you are ready, let's pick up some bricks and start building our walls.

Fortification Step 1: Identifying Breaches

When Nehemiah set out to rebuild the wall around Jerusalem, he knew he would never succeed without the sovereign intervention and aid of the Most High God. It was an impossible task. And only God could accomplish it. The same is true of the fortification of our spiritual lives. Only with God's supernatural assistance can we successfully build walls of defense against the enemy. But we cannot expect God to come to our aid if we have barriers of sin and rebellion standing in the way. God hastens to the help of those who are humble and contrite before Him.

> If My people who are called by My name will humble them-
> selves, and pray and seek My face, and turn from their wicked
> ways, then I will hear from heaven, and will forgive their sin and
> heal their land (2 Chronicles 7:14).

> The sacrifices of God are a broken spirit, a broken and a contrite
> heart—these, O God, You will not despise (Psalm 51:17).

The first thing Nehemiah did, even before attempting to lay the first brick in the wall, was to fast, pray, and repent of Israel's sins (see Nehemiah 1:6-9).

The reason that the wall around Jerusalem was in such disrepair was because the children of Israel had turned from God. They had allowed their hearts to be wooed by other gods and they had forsaken their covenant with the King of all kings. And with every step of rebellion toward God, the supernatural protection that fortified their city eroded until their wall lay in ruins and they were captured by their enemies.

During my personal fortification process, the first thing I did was pray. I asked God to show me the "breaches" in my spiritual wall. Was there anything I was allowing into my life, no matter how small, that was providing the enemy access? After several weeks of prayer and seeking God, He opened my eyes to the access points that I had given Satan, even without realizing it.

By wasting my time and money on the ungodliness of Hollywood, watching movies that glorified sin and darkness, listening to workout music that exalted sensuality, and reading magazines that promoted materialism (no matter how subtle these things were), I had unwittingly participated in the kingdom of darkness instead of the kingdom of light and, thus, had given the enemy access to my spiritual life. By habitually giving in to stress and drivenness regarding book deadlines and ministry projects, I had been leaning upon my own efforts instead of the Spirit of God and, again had given the enemy access to my spiritual life. By giving into fear about my health (especially after the miscarriage) and seeking advice from secular books that only promoted worry and paranoia, I had been agreeing with the kingdom of darkness instead of the kingdom of light and, yet again, had given the enemy access to my spiritual life.

Like Nehemiah, I repented of all these things before God and asked His Spirit to take back all access I had given to the enemy and to cleanse these sins from my life. Much like the "house-cleaning" process I described in *Authentic Beauty,* I threw away movies, books, and music that promoted worldliness, materialism, or fear—even if it was only in a small measure. I wanted no trace of the kingdom of darkness in my life. I asked God to retrain my daily habits in ministry; to remove my Martha-like attitude and make me into a Mary who sat at His feet. I asked Him to replace my fear with mighty faith in Him.

Lovingly and faithfully He helped me close off all enemy access points. As my breaches were identified and dealt with, I found that my prayers were more effective, the Word of God was more alive, and my intimacy with Christ was more vibrant. Instead of constantly warding off enemy attacks, I now had two hands free to begin rebuilding the wall around my spiritual life.

If you sense the need for spiritual fortification, the first step is to identify any enemy access points in your life. Where is your wall broken and full of breaches, allowing Satan to freely come in and pester you? Ask God's Spirit to reveal any and all enemy access points. If you seek Him with a truly open and willing heart, He will show you every hole in your wall that needs restoring. In the last chapter, we talked about letting go of worldly allurements and attractions. Often, these are the biggest breaches in our lives, and we unwittingly participate in the enemy's kingdom without even realizing it.

A close friend of mine was really struggling with spiritual attacks upon her life, waking up with horrible nightmares and battling fearful, irrational thoughts on a nearly-constant basis. One afternoon as we met together for prayer, she casually mentioned that she'd just come from a movie. When she told me which one she'd seen, I was taken aback. It was a horror/suspense film, and though it was one of the "milder" ones, it still was all about demonic darkness and death. She was completely blind to the fact that opening her mind up to those sights, sounds, and images was leaving a gaping breach in her life through which the enemy could gain access. Paul said, "Whatever things are true, whatever things are noble, whatever things are just, whatever things are pure, whatever things are lovely, whatever things are of good report, if there is any virtue and if there is anything praiseworthy—meditate on these things" (Phillippians 4:8).

When we allow our minds to dwell on darkness and death (instead of the things listed in Phillippians), doesn't it stand to reason that we invite the prince of darkness and death into our minds? It's a bit like sitting outside on a muggy Minnesota evening covered in sugar water instead of bug spray. You might as well hang a sign on your forehead that says "Mosquitoes welcome here!" And when we bathe our thoughts in evil instead of good, we might as well hang a sign over the door of our minds that says, "Darkness welcome here!"

If we watch movies and TV shows that promote sensuality, we open the door for lust and sexual compromise to waltz right into our lives. If we read magazines that feed the selfish cravings of our flesh, we open the door for materialism to take root within our souls. If we feed upon pop-culture messages, we open the door for selfishness and worldliness to gain a foothold in us.

God says we are to give no "opportunity" to the devil (see Ephesians 4:27). Removing the breaches in our walls means removing all opportunity for Satan to access our hearts and minds. That is how we will be turned from fearful closet Christians into mighty Gladys Aylward–like warriors for Christ's kingdom.

If you have begun to allow Christ's Spirit to transform the areas we mentioned in the last chapter, then you have already started to seal up breaches in your spiritual life. As you continue the process of becoming spiritually fortified, here are some other potential "breach" areas to prayerfully take before God.

Past Sins. If there are sins in your past that you have never allowed God to forgive, cleanse, and remove from you as far as the east is from the west, then you are giving permission to the accuser (Satan) to hold them over your head and pester you with guilt and condemnation. You are also leaving a barrier between you and unhindered intimacy with Christ. I would encourage you to walk through the "Cleaning the Sanctuary" guide on the website www.setapartgirl.com to help you identify and cleanse your heart of past sins. And remember, once you have brought a sin to Christ and asked His forgiveness, He removes it from you *as far away as the east is from the west* (see Psalm 103). If the enemy ever tries to hold it over your head again, stand firmly upon the reality of Christ's work on the cross. His blood has fully and completely covered that sin, and it is *no longer a part of your life.* When God looks at you, He does not see that sin. The enemy has no power or authority to torment you about a sin that is nailed to the cross. As the lyrics from the old hymn "It Is Well with My Soul" read, "My sin—O the bliss of this glorious thought—my sin, not in part but the whole, is nailed to the cross and I bear it no more, praise the Lord, it is well with my soul!"

Sinful Strongholds. If you habitually give way to sin in your life and allow it to have control over you (lust, self-pity, pride, jealously, unforgiveness, or addictions), you are creating an access point for the enemy. Ask the Spirit of God to help you recognize any habitual sin in your life. Ask Him to forgive you and to reclaim the territory that the enemy had claimed. Then allow Him to retrain you and remake you. You may feel helpless against sin's tyranny, but the power of Christ in you is far greater than the power of sin. His grace is more than sufficient to grant you complete victory and deliverance from any sinful stronghold. It can be very helpful to have an accountability partner who you meet with regularly for prayer and encouragement as you allow God to set you free from habitual sin. And if you haven't already done so, I would encourage you to read *Authentic Beauty*. It goes into greater detail about the practical side of overcoming sinful patterns in your life.

Satanic Objects or Activities. Deuteronomy 18:10-13 says, "There shall not be found among you anyone who…practices witchcraft, or a soothsayer, or one who interprets omens, or a sorcerer, or one who conjures spells, or a medium, or a spiritist, or one who calls up the dead. For all who do these things are an abomination to the LORD."

Most of us who have grown up in church don't consider ourselves vulnerable to witchcraft or Satan worship. But sometimes we overlook things that seem "harmless" but are, in reality, associated with the kingdom of darkness. Anything that we allow into our lives that is associated with witchcraft or the occult opens a wide door for the enemy to gain access to our hearts, minds, and bodies and to block the spiritual blessings Christ has for us. Something as seemingly innocent as reading your horoscope in the newspaper is actually not innocent at all—it is participating in the occult practice of fortune telling. Movies about séances or communicating with dead people might seem like no big deal—especially if you "don't really believe in them." But watching those movies is, in essence, participating in the occult practice of "calling up the dead." Even having satanic or occult objects in your home can open up a breach for the enemy to have access.

I recently read the story of Derek Prince, an English Bible scholar who was given a present from his grandfather—a set of four embroidered dragons from China. He proudly displayed them on his living room wall because they were both beautiful and held sentimental value to him. But around the time that he brought the dragons into his house, he began to sense a spiritual opposition in his ministry. He wrote, "I encountered barriers of communication that had never been there before with people close to me. Others on whom I had been relying failed to keep their commitments. A substantial legacy from my mother's estate was delayed interminably by a lawyer's inefficiency."

At first he didn't make any connection between the dragons and the spiritual attacks on his life.

But one day, as he was fasting and praying about his situation, his attention was drawn to the dragons on his wall. He realized that in Scripture, Satan was represented as a dragon. He thought, "Is it appropriate for me, as a servant of Christ, to display in my home objects that typify Christ's great adversary, Satan?" He read a passage in Deuteronomy which further opened his eyes. "You shall burn the carved images of their gods with fire. You shall not covet the silver or gold that is on them, nor take it for yourselves...nor shall you bring an abomination into your house, lest you be doomed to destruction like it. You shall utterly detest it and utterly abhor it, for it is an accursed thing" (Deuteronomy 7:25-26).

Derek wrote, "My embroidered dragons were not carved images, but they certainly were images of a false god who had been worshiped for millennia in China. By bringing them into my home, I had unknowingly exposed myself and my family to (enemy access)."[11] When Derek destroyed the dragons, he began to see a dramatic change. There was a lifting of the attacks over his life and ministry, and he experienced the blessings of God in a much more tangible way.

As we discussed in the last chapter, there can be no fellowship between light and darkness (see 2 Corinthians 6:14). Whenever we invite anything of darkness into our lives, no matter how small or harmless it may seem, we open breaches for the enemy to gain access, and we create barriers that block the blessings of Christ. In the book of Acts when the Gospel of Christ was preached, those who believed "came and openly confessed their evil deeds. A number who had practiced sorcery brought their scrolls together and burned them publicly" (Acts 19:18-19).

If there is any object or activity in our lives that is associated with witchcraft or the occult, the appropriate way to deal with it is to destroy it completely, as they did in Acts. I would encourage you to ask God to reveal to you anything in your life (past or present) that is associated with satanic activity. Here is a brief list of some things that fall into that category: horoscopes, hypnosis, palm reading, tarot cards, ouija boards, zodiac charms, fortune-telling (yes, even fortune cookies), pagan paraphernalia (like Buddha statues), clothes or jewelry with skeletons, skulls, or monsters, and anything that promotes superstition, witchcraft, séances, and the like.

Don't exclude movies, music, and books from this list—even if the movies are seemingly lighthearted (like the Will Farrell remake of *Bewitched*). Anything that tinkers with spiritual power (outside of the power of God) falls into this dangerous category. This would also include TV shows (*Charmed, Buffy the Vampire Slayer, Angel, The X-Files,* and so forth). The shows might be ridiculous and you might not take them seriously, but they still display messages of darkness and ungodly spiritual powers. Once these breaches are identified in your life, they must be removed and destroyed. Ask God to forgive you for allowing these things into your life and to reclaim any territory that was given to the enemy as a result.

Fortification Step 2: Making a Sacred List

As Eric and I embarked upon our spiritual fortification process, we made a "sacred list" of areas we felt needed special attention. We spent some time thinking about the areas in which we felt most "pestered" by the enemy or continually tempted toward compromise, and we decided to spend a season of our lives aggressively praying that those breaches would be sealed. There were many things that went onto our sacred list. There were patterns in our lives that needed to be shifted, such as our computers breaking down during a crucial writing project, habitually feeling tired and groggy during important family times, and health issues—like migraine headaches—that repeatedly flared up during seasons of intensive ministry. There were weaknesses in our lives that needed to be obliterated—such as a tendency toward worry and frustration. Anything in our lives, no matter how small, that was not a glorious, triumphant reflection of Christ went onto our list. Rather than accepting those breaches as normal, we decided to aggressively fight until a wall of fortification was completed and the enemy no longer had access to those areas.

As you pursue spiritual fortification, it can be extremely helpful to create your own "sacred list." Take some time to prayerfully consider any and all areas of your life that don't reflect the glory and triumph of Jesus Christ. For instance, if you struggle with self-pity or depression, put that on your list. If you don't sleep well at night, add that to the list. If there are people in your life that you have difficulty getting along with, put them on your list. If there is a health or financial issue that causes stress and distraction, add it to your list. If there are fears that continually haunt you, put them on your list.

Many of us assume that a life full of problems and conflicts is normal. But as we discussed earlier, we are not to accept any weakness or challenge that does not bring glory to the name of Christ. Rather, we are to aggressively fight until those breaches are sealed and we become a fortified, valiant, set-apart Proverbs 31 woman—not preoccupied with our own problems, but strong and vibrant so that we can give to those in need around us. That is not to say that challenges will never come our way. (As we discussed in the last chapter, *all those who live godly in Christ Jesus will be persecuted!*) But let's make sure we are accepting the *right kind* of challenges and the *right kind* of persecution—the healthy, fruitful, loving discipline of our King who makes us mighty for battle rather than the life-draining, debilitating attacks of the enemy that render us useless for serving Christ's kingdom.

Fortification Step 3: Wrestling Until Break of Day

It has been said by many great Christians that prayer is our secret weapon. If we desire to be free from every enemy stronghold over our lives and fully fortified to live the superhuman existences God intended us to live, *then we must learn how to pray.* As the book of Nehemiah vividly shows, fortification *will not happen* without prayer.

No one can believe how powerful prayer is and what it can
effect, except those who have learned it by experience. Whenever I have prayed earnestly, I have been heard and have
obtained more than I prayed for. God sometimes delays, but
He always comes.

—MARTIN LUTHER

There is no power like that of prevailing prayer—of Abraham
pleading for Sodom, Jacob wrestling in the stillness of the night,
Moses standing in the breach, Hannah intoxicated with sorrow,
David heartbroken with remorse and grief, Jesus in sweat of
blood. Such prayer prevails. It turns ordinary mortals into men
of power. It brings power. It brings fire. It brings rain. It brings
life. It brings God.[12]

—SAMUEL CHADWICK

Though I have spent years writing and speaking about intimacy
with Christ, when God began to teach me about fortification, I was
startled to realize how little I understood about prayer. When I spent
time in Christ's presence, I had learned how to worship Him, study
His Word, let Him speak to me through stories of great Christians,
and journal my thoughts, fears, and praises as prayers to Him. But
the idea of *wrestling, importunate, persistent* prayer was completely
foreign to me. Whenever I had a specific request, concern, or need, I
brought it to Christ—once or twice. Instead of praying with confidence and boldness, I prayed, "Lord, if it is Your will, then please do
this or that." And if no answer came after one or two times of praying,
usually I just assumed that it wasn't "His will" to answer, and I let it
go. It even seemed unspiritual to keep pressing the issue with God.
I felt that it was better to just cheerfully accept the lack of response
from heaven, rather than act like a pesky child and go back to Him
again and again.

But then I started studying what Scripture says about prayer. And what I found was somewhat shocking. Take a look at what Christ teaches about prayer.

He asks us to be relentlessly persistent.

> Which of you shall have a friend, and go to him at midnight and say to him, "Friend, lend me three loaves for a friend of mine has come to me on his journey, and I have nothing to set before him"; and he will answer from within and say, "Do not trouble me; the door is now shut, and my children are with me in bed; I cannot rise and give to you"? I say to you, though he will not rise and give to him because he is his friend, yet because of his persistence he will rise and give him as many as he needs. So I say to you, ask, and it will be given to you; seek, and you will find; knock, and it will be opened to you. For everyone who asks receives, and he who seeks finds, and to him who knocks it will be opened (Luke 11:5-9).

> Then He spoke a parable to them, that men always ought to pray and not lose heart, saying: "There was in a certain city a judge who did not fear God nor regard man. Now there was a widow in that city; and she came to him, saying, 'Get justice for me from my adversary.' And he would not for a while; but afterward he said within himself, 'Though I do not fear God nor regard man, yet because this widow troubles me I will avenge her, lest by her continual coming she weary me.'" Then the Lord said, "Hear what the unjust judge said. And shall God not avenge His own elect who cry out day and night to Him, though He bears long with them? I tell you He will avenge them speedily" (Luke18:1-8).

> Most assuredly, I say to you, whatever you ask the Father in My name He will give you. Until now you have asked nothing in My name. Ask, and you will receive, that your joy may be full (John 16:23-24).

> Be anxious for nothing, but in everything by prayer and supplication, with thanksgiving, let your requests be made known to God (Phillippians 4:6).

Look at this remarkable story of one woman's persistence in seeking Christ's healing for her daughter:

> And behold, a woman of Canaan came from that region and cried out to Him, saying, "Have mercy on me, O Lord, Son of David! My daughter is severely demon-possessed." But He answered her not a word. And His disciples came and urged Him, saying, "Send her away, for she cries out after us." But He answered and said, "I was not sent except to the lost sheep of the house of Israel." Then she came and worshiped Him, saying, "Lord, help me!" But He answered and said, "It is not good to take the children's bread and throw it to the little dogs." And she said, "Yes, Lord, yet even the little dogs eat the crumbs which fall from their masters' table." Then Jesus answered and said to her, "O woman, great is your faith! Let it be to you as you desire." And her daughter was healed from that very hour (Matthew 15:11-28).

What an incredible picture of the kind of persistence Christ requires in our prayers! Instead of rebuking the woman for pestering Him relentlessly, He praises her tireless faith and answers her petition.

E.M. Bounds wrote an insightful observation about this story:

> The case of the Syrophoenician woman…is a notable instance of successful importunity (persistence)…At first, Jesus appears to

pay no attention to her agony, and ignores her cry for relief. He gives neither eye, nor ear, nor word. Silence, deep and chilling, greets her impassioned cry. But she is not turned aside, nor disheartened. She holds on. The disciples, offended at her unseemly clamor, intercede for her, but are silenced by the Lord's declaring that the woman is entirely outside the scope of His mission and His ministry. But neither the failure of the disciples to gain her a hearing nor the knowledge—despairing in its very nature—that she is barred from the benefits of His mission, daunt her, and serve only to lend intensity and increased boldness to her approach to Christ. She came closer...falling at His feet, worshiping Him and making her daughter's case her own cries, with pointed brevity, "Lord, help me!" This last cry won her case; her daughter was healed in the self-same hour. Hopeful, urgent and unwearied, she stays near the master, insisting and praying until the answer is given. What a study in importunity, in earnestness, in persistence, promoted and propelled under conditions which would have disheartened any but a heroic, constant soul. (Jesus) teaches that an answer to prayer is conditional upon the amount of faith that goes to the petition. To test this, He delays the answer. The superficial pray-er subsides into silence, when the answer is delayed. But the man of prayer hangs on, and on. The Lord recognizes and honors his faith, and gives him a rich and abundant answer to His faith evidencing, importunate prayer.[13]

Instead of assuming that Christ doesn't desire to answer our prayers when we don't receive an immediate response, we are to press in with even more persistence, *not letting go* until our request is granted. Just as Jacob wrestled all night with God saying, "I will not let You go until You bless me," we are to wrestle in prayer until the breaking of day (see Genesis 32:26).

E.M. Bounds said it well: "He prays not at all who does not press his plea."[14] If there is a problem in your life that you can't seem to overcome, don't waste your time complaining, analyzing, or talking about it. Take it to God in importunate prayer. Wrestle until the breaking of day. And remember, as Martin Luther said, "God may delay, but He always comes."

> Our praying needs to be pressed and pursued with an energy that never tires, a persistency which will not be denied, and a courage that never fails.[15]
>
> —E.M. BOUNDS

He delights to give good gifts to His children.

I have often told young women, "God cares more about your desire for a beautiful love story than even you do!" For some reason, it is easier for us to imagine God wanting to make us miserable than wanting to bless us. I used to fear that if I allowed Him to write my love story, I would end up with someone I wasn't at all attracted to. Instead, as I gave the pen to the Author of romance, He wrote a fairy tale story more beautiful than anything I could ever have hoped for. That's the way God works. When we are fully yielded to Him, He *delights* to give us good and perfect gifts.

> Ask, and it will be given to you; seek, and you will find; knock, and it will be opened to you. For everyone who asks receives, and he who seeks finds, and to him who knocks it will be opened. Or what man is there among you who, if his son asks for bread, will give him a stone? Or if he asks for a fish, will he give him a serpent? If you then, being evil, know how to give good gifts to your children, how much more will your Father who is in heaven give good things to those who ask Him! (Matthew 7:7-11).

> Consider the lilies how they grow: they toil not, they spin not; and yet I say unto you, that Solomon in all his glory was not arrayed

like one of these. If then God so clothe the grass, which is to day in the field, and to morrow is cast into the oven; how much more will he clothe you, O ye of little faith? Fear not, little flock; for it is your Father's good pleasure to give you the kingdom (Luke 12:27-28,32).

Every good gift and every perfect gift is from above, and comes down from the Father of lights, with whom there is no variation or shadow of turning (James 1:17).

The LORD will give grace and glory; no good thing will He withhold from those who walk uprightly (Psalm 84:11).

Many of us are afraid to pray about things we need or desire, because we think that we are praying to a scowling Master who is far more interested in discipline than in love. But the entire reason He came to earth was for love. He longs to bless us beyond what we could ever think or imagine. And when we submit our lives fully and completely to Him, we have access to all the benefits that He purchased for us on the cross. We are not to forget those benefits, but to *receive* them and *rejoice* in them:

Bless the LORD, O my soul, and forget not all His benefits, who forgives all your iniquities, who heals all your diseases, who redeems your life from destruction, who crowns you with lovingkindness and tender mercies, who satisfies your mouth with good things, so that your youth is renewed like the eagle's (Psalm 103:2-5).

It is common to pray, "Lord, if it is Your will, do this or that." But often this keeps us from being bold and specific in our praying. If we are always unsure whether we are praying in accordance with His will, then we will not have the confidence to wrestle until the break of day. It is true that we must pray in alignment with His will to receive answers. But we often overlook the fact that anything that is in alignment with His nature is in accordance with His will. We don't need to wonder whether or not God wants to give us freedom from sin, power over the enemy, perfect peace, exceeding joy, health, strong relationships, a beautiful marriage, and fruitfulness in His kingdom. These are things He makes very clear in Scripture that He delights to give us. (And the more we learn to listen to the still, small voice of His Spirit, the more we learn what His will is even in regard to the specific details of our lives. No longer do we merely pray our own prayers, but we pray the things that are on His heart to pray, in agreement with His Spirit. See Romans 8:26.)

To be honest, it makes me a little uncomfortable to make such bold statements about the manifold blessings of God because I have seen many professing Christians abuse this principle, asking God to give them the selfish cravings of their flesh. (Like the "name-it, claim-it" people who think that if they ask in faith for a Lamborghini, God will give it to them.) Scripture makes it clear that if we are living for selfish pleasure instead of for Christ, we will not receive the things we ask for. "You ask and do not receive, because you ask amiss, that you may spend it on your pleasures" (James 4:3).

But if we have yielded our entire hearts, minds, and bodies to the Spirit of Christ, and are allowing Him to have rulership over our lives, we can be confident that He desires to give us "everything we need for life and godliness" (see 2 Peter 1:3). He gives us good gifts, not so that we can keep the benefits of His kingdom to ourselves, but so that we are strong enough to pour them out on behalf of people in need. He blesses us so that we can be a blessing to others.

> I will bless you and make your name great; and you shall be a blessing (Genesis 12:22).

> And God is able to make all grace abound toward you, that you, always having all sufficiency in all things, may have an abundance for every good work (2 Corinthians 9:8).

If you ever hesitate to bring your requests to God, remember that He is a loving Father. Just watching Eric's pleasure in meeting our children's daily needs for love, affection, food, clothes, sleep, and so forth makes me realize how much God enjoys blessing *us* with His good gifts. He goes above and beyond our expectations. As Martin Luther said, "Whenever I have prayed earnestly, I have always received more than I have asked for." When we ask our Father for bread, He will not give us a stone.

He wants us to ask for big things—and have faith that He will answer.

> Jesus answered and said to them, "Assuredly, I say to you, if you have faith and do not doubt...if you say to this mountain, 'Be removed and be cast into the sea,' it will be done. And whatever things you ask in prayer, believing, you will receive (Matthew 21:21).

> Most assuredly, I say to you, he who believes in Me, the works that I do he will do also; and greater works than these he will do, because I go to My Father. And whatever you ask in My name, that I will do, that the Father may be glorified in the Son. If you ask anything in My name, I will do it (John 14:12-14).

Again I say to you that if two of you agree on earth concerning anything that they ask, it will be done for them by My Father in heaven. For where two or three are gathered together in My name, I am there in the midst of them (Matthew 18:19-20).

Jesus said to him, "...all things are possible to him who believes" (Mark 9:23).

The effective, fervent prayer of a righteous man avails much. Elijah was a man with a nature like ours, and he prayed earnestly that it would not rain; and it did not rain on the land for three years and six months. And he prayed again, and the heavens gave rain, and the earth produced its fruit (James 5:16-18).

God honors not wisdom nor personality, but faith. Faith honors God. And God honors faith. God goes wherever faith puts Him. Faith links our impotence to His omnipotence. Doubt delays and often destroys faith. Faith destroys doubt.[16]

—LEONARD RAVENHILL

God asks us to have the kind of faith that asks boldly for specific things. Instead of vague, general prayers that don't demand faith, we must begin "putting it all on the line" and take the risk of laying our precise needs before our King. Charles Spurgeon said, "There is a general kind of praying which fails for lack of precision. It is as if a regiment of soldiers should all fire off their guns anywhere. Possibly somebody would be killed, but the majority of the enemy would be missed."

The set-apart women of history past were rich in faith—and their expectations of God were enormous. Catherine Booth, the young wife and mother who cofounded the world-altering Salvation Army movement with her husband, described one of her first acts of "stepping out in faith" for the work of God:

> I observed a woman standing on the adjoining doorstep with a jug in her hand. My divine teacher said, "Speak to that woman." After a momentary struggle I introduced myself to her and invited her [to the church service]. She answered, "I can't go to chapel, I am kept at home by a drunken husband." I asked if I might come in and see her husband. "No" she said. "He is drunk; you could do nothing with him, and he will only abuse you." I replied, "I am not afraid; he will not hurt me." I followed her up the stairs. I felt strong now in the Lord and in the power of His might, and as safe as a babe in the arms of its mother. I realized I was in the path of obedience, and I feared no evil.
>
> I found a fine, intelligent man, about forty, sitting almost double in a chair, with a jug by his side, out of which he had been drinking. I leaned on my heavenly Guide for strength and wisdom, love and power and He gave me all I needed. He silenced the demon, strong drink, and quickened the man's perceptions to receive my words. As I began to talk to him, with my heart full of sympathy, he gradually raised himself in his chair, and listened with a surprised and half-vacant stare. I spoke to him of his present deplorable condition, of the folly and wickedness of his course, of the interest of his wife and children, until he was fully aroused from the stupor in which I found him. I read to him the parable of the Prodigal Son, while the tears ran down his face like rain. I then prayed as the Spirit gave me utterance, and left, promising to call the next day.

From that time I commenced a systematic course of house-to-house visitation, devoting two evenings per week to the work. The Lord so blessed my efforts that in a few weeks I succeeded in getting ten drunkards to abandon their soul-destroying habits and to meet me once a week for reading the Scriptures and for prayer.[17]

Catherine's decision to ask big things of her Lord and stand upon the promise that "all things are possible with God" laid the foundation for one of the most powerful, world-impacting ministries that has ever been. She and her husband labored to be Christ's hands and feet to the afflicted, downtrodden, and forgotten, more than any other Christians in their generation. And because of her huge faith in a huge God, she saw the Salvation Army develop from a humble Christian mission in London to one of the largest Christian forces in the world, literally impacting millions for the Gospel of Christ.

One of Amy Carmichael's earliest ministry acts was to boldly ask God for something that other Christians would not even consider asking for. As a young missionary she went to speak about Christ to a pagan, Japanese village. Before going, she wrestled fervently in prayer, feeling pressed to ask God for eight souls to be won that night for His kingdom. She described it as an "irresistible divine pressure to ask and receive, according to 1 John 5:14-15. This is the confidence that we have in Him, that if we ask anything according to his will, He hears us. And if we know that He hears us, whatever we ask, we know that we have the petitions that we have asked of him."

Amy asked her fellow missionaries to join her in asking God for eight souls at the meeting—a far greater number than had ever been won. They resisted being so bold in their requests of God, saying "if we ask for something we don't receive, it will bring shame to the name of Christ!" But, in the midst of all the unbelief that swirled around her, Amy had no doubt that God wanted to give eight souls. She prayed intensely, believing that it would be done, and God rewarded her faith by giving her exactly what she asked for.[18]

Amy's bold step of "asking and receiving" laid the foundation for a world-shaping ministry based not on the ingenuity of men, but upon the power of God. At a time when other Christians looked the other way as countless children were forced into temple prostitution, Amy went boldly into the thick of the battle and rescued over a thousand of these little ones, raising them for the kingdom of heaven.

Gladys Aylward's faith in God was so strong that she willingly walked into the middle of a bloody prison riot, where men were clubbing and killing each other. The guards had given up trying to restore order. But Gladys simply depended upon the faithfulness and power of her King. Standing in the midst of the violence, she commanded them to stop and be quiet. Instantly, a change came over all of the men. They put down their weapons and walked obediently back to their cells. The guards came in, astounded to find every prisoner sitting meekly and quietly in his own cell.[19]

When Hudson Taylor was a wayward teen with no real interest in God, his mother labored diligently in prayer on his behalf, full of faith that God would hear and answer. One day, when she was away from home staying with a friend, she felt especially pressed to wrestle in prayer for his soul. She knelt by her bed and determined not to rise from the spot until she was confident that her son's soul had been won for Christ. Hour after hour she pleaded for Hudson, until at last she could pray no longer, but knew in her heart that the victory had been gained. Christ's Spirit made it clear to her that her son had come into the kingdom of God that very day. Upon her arrival home several days later, Hudson met her at the door to tell her the joyful news that he had given his life to Christ the very same afternoon that she had wrestled for him in prayer.[20]

Our generation of Christians hasn't seen much of the power of God, at least in the mainstream Western world. We assume that all the incredible miracles done by Christians in the book of Acts were for a "different time." In the early church, the blind received sight, the dead were raised, the enemies of God were struck dead, and prison doors miraculously opened. God doesn't seem to operate the same with His children today, and many theologians have concocted elaborate doctrines to explain why God's power isn't to be expected in our modern times. But James said, "You do not have because you do not ask" (James 4:2). The conquering power of God is available to any of His children who have faith enough to ask for it.

> The greatest old or new testament saints were on a level that is quite within our reach. The same spiritual power that enabled them to become our spiritual heroes, is also available to us.[21]
>
> —EDWARD MEYRICK GOULBURN

What keeps us from receiving this "power from on high"? John Wesley said it well: "Have you any days of fasting and prayer? Storm the throne of grace and mercy will come down."

God is looking for the next generation of Catherine Booths, Amy Carmichaels, and Gladys Aylwards. He is calling you to be among the ranks of set-apart women who believe that He will be as big as He says He is—and usher in the power of God through powerful praying.

He asks us to pray "day and night" without ceasing.

> O brother, pray; in spite of Satan, pray; spend hours in prayer; rather neglect friends than not pray; rather fast, and lose breakfast, dinner, tea, and supper—and sleep too—than not pray. And we must not talk about prayer, we must pray in right earnest. The Lord is near. He comes softly while the virgins slumber.
>
> —ANDREW BONAR

Paul exhorted us to "pray without ceasing" (1 Thessalonians 5:17). Most Christians refuse to take that statement literally, saying, "Well, obviously, he didn't really mean that we need to pray 24 hours a day! How unrealistic!"

But all through Scripture, God bestows great honor upon those who seek Him *day and night*. At the time of Christ's birth, there was a woman named Anna who lived in the temple. She "did not depart from the temple, but served God with fastings and prayers night and day" (Luke 2:37). When Mary and Joseph brought Christ to the temple as a baby, Anna instantly knew He was the Son of God and spoke of Him to all who awaited the redemption of Israel.

Did Anna have a "special call" upon her life for prayer? Or is that kind of continual, fervent prayer the call of *every* set-apart woman of God? The New Testament describes the characteristics of a "virtuous widow" who is qualified to receive help from believers. This woman's description seems to parallel the miraculous, poured-out life portrayed by the Proverbs 31 woman. She does not live for her own pleasure but is well reported for good works, bringing up children, lodging strangers, washing the saints' feet, relieving the afflicted, and diligently following every good work. How does she accomplish all of this? "She trusts in God and continues in *supplications and prayers night and day*" (I Timothy 5:5-6,10). She lives a supernatural existence, accomplishing incredible things without stress and exhaustion because *she makes prayer the foundation of her life.*

Remember that depressing book description of the woman whose life is a study in disappointment?

> You once dreamed of a life of Prince Charmings and fairy-tale endings. But now that you've grown up and arrived at womanhood, those dreams seem so far out of reach. Your husband isn't quite the guy you thought you married, your kids face challenges you never dreamed of, you have to work a lot more than you expected just to make ends meet, your spiritual life is a joke, and even the bedroom wallpaper you saved up for just looks wrong.[22]

Contrary to what the book implies, this woman is not a victim to disappointing circumstances. There is a telling line in that paragraph that perfectly explains why her life is such a mess. It says that her "spiritual life is a joke." If our spiritual life is a joke, if prayer is nonexistent, and if Christ is squeezed into random corners of our day, then we are susceptible to every pestering problem the enemy could throw our way—marriage and family disintegration, relational conflicts, financial frustration, depression, sickness, discouragement, and so forth.

But when our spiritual lives are thriving, when prayer is the foundation of our existence, every other area of our lives begins to thrive as a result. Not only will we have victory in our personal lives, we will be strong in order to pour out on behalf of others, like the virtuous women in 1 Timothy 5 and in Proverbs 31. In Matthew 6:33, Christ says that when we seek first His kingdom and His righteousness, *all* the things we need will be supernaturally added to us.

Conventional wisdom and common sense tell us that it is unrealistic to make seeking God's kingdom the centerpiece of our lives. But God's ways don't typically line up with conventional wisdom or common sense. The principles of His kingdom seem ridiculous to the natural human mind. That's why most of us spend more time reasoning about God's Word than actually obeying it.

When God first challenged Eric and me to fight for spiritual fortification, we realized that we needed to make fervent prayer the *highest priority* of our day. We had always made prayer a part of our lives, but now we felt challenged to make our lives all about prayer. We began to pray intensely for two or three hours every morning, and at least an hour in the evening. Some nights we wrestled in prayer for five, six, or even seven hours until 3:00 or 4:00 in the morning. And many weeks we devoted an entire day out of the week to fasting and importunate prayer.

We prayed while we were driving down the road. We prayed while we were getting ready in the morning. We prayed when our kids woke up crying in the middle of the night. We prayed when we were making dinner. We prayed when we were taking walks or riding our bikes. We prayed as we were drifting off to sleep at night. We prayed before we even got out of bed in the morning. We prayed while we were writing our books. We prayed with everyone who came into our home. We visited friends and neighbors in need and prayed for them. We met together with our church community and prayed regularly. More and more, we began to learn what it means to "pray without ceasing."

We have continued this pattern for almost two years, and in the midst of it, we have written four full-length books, presented more than 200 hours of public speaking, launched two major websites, conducted countless media interviews and conference calls, gone on several trips, pastored a church community, personally mentored several young people each week, helped our two-year-old memorize 180 country flags and capitals, the solar system, and 140 dog breeds, and adopted a five-month-old baby girl from Korea.

Is our life frenzied, driven, and chaotic? Quite the opposite. In fact, this year has been full of romance, fun, and relaxation. Most of our neighbors probably think we live a leisurely life; we are always riding our bikes to the local malt shop, taking afternoon strolls to the park with our kids, watching the rain from our front porch, or enjoying long picnics with friends and family.

Are we worn-out and constantly craving rest? Not at all. In fact, we have never been so healthy, strong, and energetic—and we don't even drink caffeine! Even with a new baby who came with her days and nights completely mixed up and no idea how to soothe herself to sleep, we have had the unction to devote time to fervent prayer and energetically tackle all the work that God has called us to.

How is this possible? Through prayer! This year God has shown Eric and me the secret to living a "miracle" life—make prayer the foundation of our existence and everything else falls beautifully into place. Trying to live a supernatural life in our own strength has historically caused us to feel overwhelmed, stressed, and exhausted. But through prayer, we have learned to transfer our burdens onto Christ's capable shoulders. And when He carries our burdens, we are free to run and not grow weary, to walk and not faint (see Isaiah 40).

On two different occasions, the disciples fished all night long and caught absolutely nothing. But when Jesus came and stood in their midst, they merely had to let down their net once and such an abundance was caught that they didn't even have room in their boat to contain it all (see Luke 5:4-11 and John 21:3-6).

When prayer is missing from our lives, we spend countless time and energy trying to make our lives work, constantly failing and beating our heads against the wall in frustration. But as it says in Psalm 1, when we meditate upon our Lord day and night, we become like a tree that brings forth much fruit—and everything that we do *just works*. Our time is multiplied. Our effectiveness is multiplied. Our energy is multiplied. Life becomes fruitful instead of frustrating.

Recently, Eric and I shared with a group of young people about our new focus on prayer. Their response was, "Well, I would love to be able to do that, but it's just not realistic for me. I have to work, and I have friends and family who demand my time and attention." The ironic thing was that these people were young and single and had far fewer distractions and responsibilities than we did (no babies to tend to in the middle of the night, no toddlers needing attention all day, and no book deadlines looming). Yet they felt that devoting hours to prayer was impossible and unrealistic for them.

Another one said, "Well, I just don't want to spend time in prayer until I am sure it won't be legalism." Such excuses are prevalent in our generation of lazy, self-absorbed Christians. We will come up with anything and everything as a reason for staying away from God's throne of grace. (By the way, if you are worried that you might "pray out of legalism," then get on your face before God and beckon Him to enable you to yield to His Spirit instead of your own effort. The answer is not to stay away from prayer, but to aggressively seek Him until the victory is won!)

Is it not a proof that the Holy Spirit is a stranger in the church when prayer, for which God has made such provisions, is regarded as a task and a burden?

—ANDREW MURRAY

He who runs from God in the morning will scarcely find Him the rest of the day.

—JOHN BUNYAN

There is no substitute for prayer. Nothing will make up for the lack of it in our lives. As Leonard Ravenhill put it, "No man is greater than his prayer life. The pastor who is not praying is playing; the people who are not praying are straying. Poverty-stricken as the Church is today in many things, she is most stricken here, in the place of prayer. In the matter of New Testament, Spirit-inspired, hell-shaking, world-breaking prayer, never has so much been left to so few. For this kind of prayer there is no substitute. We do it—or we die!"[23]

I hardly think of myself as an expert on prayer. Like I said, it has only been in the past year that God has opened my eyes to the true potency of this "secret weapon." Eric and I feel that we have only just begun to experience the heights and depths of wrestling, importunate prayer. We fully expect to continue learning and growing in this area for the rest of our lives. But one thing that I can say for certain is that I have never seen so much answered prayer in my life as this year, when I have devoted myself to continual fervent, specific, bold praying.

When we found out that our baby's adoption from Korea would probably take six to eight months (normally it takes two years, but because she was a "waiting child" with special needs, the process was faster), I began to pray daily that her adoption would be the fastest one our agency had ever done. Miracles began to happen left and right.

Government forms that normally took ten weeks were processed in seven days. Paperwork that usually takes months sailed through the red tape. When we got the call saying that she was ready to be picked up from Korea after *less than three months,* the agency said, "This has to be the fastest adoption our agency has ever done!" There was no other explanation than the supernatural power of God. Out of thousands of adoptions—ours was the fastest ever. Why? Because we laid a bold, specific request before our Lord, and He faithfully answered. This is just one of many incredible miracles we've seen since we began building our life around prayer.

And by the way, God has a beautiful way of turning to good everything the enemy means for evil in our lives. Our daughter's arrival lined up almost perfectly with the due date for the baby we lost. Through prayer, He turned my "weeping into dancing." If there is an area in which the enemy has defeated you, pray diligently that God would redeem it fully and completely. And then watch to see the beauty of His ways! It's a prayer He delights to answer.

How do you begin to add this kind of fervent prayer into your life? Don't get bogged down with complicated formulas. Don't wait until prayer seems convenient. And, as Corrie ten Boom said, "Don't pray when you feel like it. Have an appointment with the Lord and keep it."

When it comes to prayer, the best advice I can give is—*just do it!* Build prayer into every corner of your life. Even if you have to lose sleep or miss a meal, make prayer the highest priority of your day.

Whether you go outside into God's creation and pray silently, or go into your closet and cry out to Him at the top of your voice, you will learn how to pray more powerfully the more you put it into practice. It may feel awkward and tedious at first. The first time that Eric and I attempted to spend an entire day in prayer, the hours seemed to drag. But now, I would rather be praying than doing just about anything else. It truly has become my delight, joy, and privilege to spend hours in God's presence through prayer.

═══════════════════════════════════════

As a full-time student, living a set-apart life means prioritizing my day. Most days I have to get up early (5:30 A.M.), even though I am not a morning person, to make time to spend with God because I know the rest of my day will be full and I will be very tired by the time I go to bed. If I do not treat my time with God like I would treat any other important commitment, I don't give God the time He deserves. If I know that I need some extra time with the Lord, I schedule it. I write in my planner, "Saturday, 9-11 A.M., prayer and study." That way I do not make my days so busy that I run out of time for God.

—Sarah, 23

═══════════════════════════════════════

Fortification Step 4: Be On Guard Against Opposition

> Men of prayer must be men of steel, for they will be assaulted by Satan even before they attempt to assault his kingdom.[24]
>
> —LEONARD RAVENHILL

When you begin to take steps forward to secure the wall around your city, you can bank on the fact that the enemy will pull out all stops to try to thwart and discourage you.

> Our enemy is more aware than we are of the spiritual possibilities that depend upon obedience. We should never be surprised that he seeks by assault and, if that fails, by undermining our defenses, to compel us to give way.[25]
>
> —AMY CARMICHAEL

When Nehemiah was in the process of building the wall around Jerusalem, the enemies of Israel did everything possible to thwart the process: "When Sanballat, Tobiah, the Arabs, the Ammonites, and the Ashdodites heard that the walls of Jerusalem were being restored and the gaps were beginning to be closed, that they became very angry, and all of them conspired together to come and attack Jerusalem and create confusion" (Nehemiah 4:7-8).

What an incredible picture of the enemy's tactic against us! Whenever we move forward in prayer, spiritual progress, or fortification, he does everything he can to create confusion. Using doubt, discouragement, and fear, he creates a "smoke and mirrors" magic show of illusion, trying to make himself appear more powerful than he really is and convince us that we will never succeed in completing the building process.

If you find that you are being constantly distracted with the cares of life, bogged down with emotional or physical "fog," or pestered with irrational thoughts and fears, there is a good chance that the enemy of your soul is attempting to create confusion and keep you from building a wall of fortification around your life. Beware of saying, "I'll press into God once these issues are gone." That's exactly how the enemy wants you to respond. Like Nehemiah, we must aggressively pray and fight until the enemy realizes that we will not kowtow to his bullying.

> Nevertheless we made our prayer to our God, and because of them we set a watch against them day and night. Therefore I positioned men behind the lower parts of the wall, at the openings; and I set the people according to their families, with their swords, their spears, and their bows. And I...said to... the people, "Do not be afraid of them. Remember the Lord, great and awesome, and fight..." And it happened, when our enemies heard that it was known to us, and that God had brought their plot to nothing, that all of us returned to the wall, everyone to his work (Nehemiah 4:9,13-15).

Christ said, "Watch and pray, lest you enter into temptation" (Matthew 26:41). Don't expect the fortification process to be easy, especially when you first begin. But if you remain constantly on guard against the enemy, setting "a watch upon your wall," and fight aggressively in prayer against all attack and confusion, then the enemy's plots will amount to absolutely nothing. Soon your wall will be completed and you will become *offensive,* rather than defensive, in the spiritual realm.

Sacred Ardor

femininity that makes marriage dreams come true

A well-known training program for Christian college students has a special emphasis on marriage and family preparation. They focus on helping young people take "realistic" expectations into marriage so that they don't become disillusioned when wedded bliss isn't everything they thought it would be. It's rather ironic when you think about it. Here is a group of Christian young people who have spent their entire life hearing that they should save sex until marriage. Christian leaders have always told them, "your marriage will be so much better if you wait!" And now the same people who heralded the many merits of "waiting" are cautioning them not to get their hopes up for a "happily ever after" love story.

Amanda is a frustrated college senior who is tired of the double standard she keeps hearing from Christians. In a recent email she wrote, "Why would I go through all the pain, loneliness, and sacrifice of keeping myself pure if I am only going to end up with a mediocre marriage anyway?"

It's a sentiment commonly shared by the younger generation of Christians. We see the dismal marriages so prevalent in our parents' generation, and we begin to wonder whether there really is anything worth waiting for after all.

This week, the front page of our local newspaper declared, "Twenty-Somethings Saying 'I Don't!' to Marriage." In today's world, marriage is quickly losing its luster. Our secular peers are chucking the whole concept of "happily ever after" in exchange for a "liberated" lifestyle of meaningless sexual encounters with random strangers. Marriage seems like nothing but a recipe for heartache and disaster, and the younger generation is beginning to avoid it like the plague. Most of us know that if our culture continues to reject God's design for marriage and family, the emotional, physical, and social ramifications will be staggering.

But are Christians helping the problem?

The Christian community constantly howls to the public about protecting the sanctity of marriage. Meanwhile Christian marriages are failing at the same rate as the rest of the world. Last week I drove by one of the "mega-churches" in our area. A huge banner hung from the side of the building so that all the interstate traffic could see it. It read: Divorce Recovery Seminar This Weekend!

How sad. Instead of showcasing the supernatural victory of Christ, this church was proudly proclaiming, "We have all the same problems as the rest of you, but at least we hold seminars about it! You should come join us!"

Christian marriages should be the *example* to the rest of the world, demonstrating that following God's ways brings abundant life, joy, peace, and supernatural victory. Instead, we are training our young people to take dismal expectations into marriage and cautioning them not to get their hopes up too high.

When Eric and I were first married, I heard a Christian psychologist on the radio say, "Every married couple, at some point in their life together, will wake up one morning, look across the table at their spouse, and wonder whether they married the right person."

I was horrified at such a thought. God had perfectly scripted my love story with Eric, and I had grown to recognize God as the true Author of romance. Why should I expect something that started out so beautiful to end up turning so sour?

I mentioned this to other married Christians and always seemed to hear the same response. "Just wait," they would tell me. "You are still a newlywed. Pretty soon the honeymoon magic will die, and you'll understand what that guy was talking about."

But Eric and I refused to give in to their dismal expectations. We were convinced that when God puts something together, it only gets *better* with time. Think about Christ's first miracle—turning water into wine at a wedding. The wedding host was astounded that the very best wine was saved until the end of the celebration. This is a profound picture of what Christ does for a marriage relationship that is centered on Him. When Jesus builds a lifelong romance between a husband and wife, He saves the best for last!

Now Eric and I have been married almost 13 years. And I can honestly say that our love story has only grown more beautiful, more romantic, and more fulfilling with every passing year. (Just this morning, I found a sweet love letter from Eric waiting for me as I sat down to write!) We have never once looked across the table from each other and wondered whether we married the right person. We have never grown disillusioned with our marriage. And we have never had our hopes dashed to pieces because our expectations were too high.

Are we merely an exception to the rule? Are we simply fortunate to have missed out on the mediocrity that seems to visit every other married couple? Absolutely not. Eric and I believe that victorious, beautiful Christian marriages are in the grasp of *everyone* who invites Jesus to be the centerpiece of their love story.

What this generation of young Christians needs is not *lower* expectations of marriage, but higher ones. We need to understand what is truly possible when the Author of lifelong love scripts the story.

Just as God has called us as young women to showcase a radiant, triumphant, super-human victory through our lives, He has called us to showcase a supernatural, lifelong, spectacular romance through our marriages. After all, the entire Bible is a picture of marriage—the love of the Bridegroom toward His bride. Christian marriages are meant to be a picture of heaven on earth.

As a set-apart young woman there are many things you can do to prepare right now for a marriage that will defy the odds.

Make Jesus Christ Your First Love

If anyone should be able to talk about the "rude awakening" that often takes place after a honeymoon, it should be me. After Eric and I rode off into the sunset to live happily ever after, reality kicked in. Our honeymoon was full of warm sunny days sipping lemonade by the pool, taking long walks, and basking in the wonder of our new life together. But after the honeymoon ended, life became a bit more challenging. Here's an excerpt from our book *When God Writes Your Love Story* that will give you a glimpse into what I mean.

> Two months into our marriage, our life looked like anything but a beautiful fairy tale come true. As with many young couples, finances were tight. We lived in a rented house in Michigan, miles away from the nearest city. In the summer, the house was used as a bed and breakfast for tourists, surrounded by gorgeous flowers and beautiful trees overlooking a shimmering lake. But in the heart of winter, when we lived there, it was a different story. The lake was frozen. The skies were gloomy. The trees were barren. The house seemed eerie and isolated, like the setting for a horror film.
>
> Whenever Eric was at work, I became desperately lonely. I was alone in the huge creepy house all day long, without a car and without a job. Since I had just moved to Michigan, I knew very few people in the area. We had no neighbors nearby. I missed my family. I missed my friends. I missed my life back in Colorado.
>
> But that was only the beginning of my woes.
>
> "I think there might be bedbugs in our mattress," I announced

to Eric one morning, scratching a patch of red bumps that had surfaced on my leg.

The house had seven bedrooms, so that night we tried sleeping in a different bed. But when morning came, I had even more red spots than before. Eric too began to notice a few itchy marks on his legs. After a week of trying out every bed in the place, we were only getting more and more covered with the strange bites. We washed the bedding, vacuumed the mattresses, and scrutinized each bed for bedbugs, but never came any closer to solving the mystery.

And then one day, my eye caught an unusual movement on the living room floor. Crouching down, I saw hundreds of tiny black spots, leaping up and down out of the carpet fibers. Our bites weren't from bedbugs; they were from fleas.

The house was infested. Horrified, I called Eric at work and told him to pick up a can of flea killer on his way home.

That night we set off a super-potent "flea bomb" that the hardware store clerk assured us would kill every flea within a two-mile radius.

It didn't work. The next day, the fleas seemed to have multiplied. All day long, they attacked me with a new vengeance. No matter where I sat in the house, within minutes my clothes would be covered with at least 50 of the disgusting insects. By this time, my arms and legs looked as if I had fallen asleep in a patch of poison ivy.

We sprayed again. And once more, the fleas seemed to only thrive on the high-octane bug killer that now permeated the air.

To make matters worse, that night I woke up with a pounding headache, coughing loud enough to rattle the windows. I was having an allergic reaction to the flea bombs.

The sub-zero weather, mixed with the harsh chemicals that filled the house, began to take its toll on my body. What started as a fit of coughing developed quickly into an alarming case of bronchitis. The doctor prescribed a regimen of antibiotics and bed rest. Within a week I had used up an entire supply closet full of Kleenex boxes.

I was lonely, sicker than I had been in years, and covered in fleabites. I was sure things couldn't get any worse.

I was wrong.

One morning as I lay on the couch shaking with a fever, I heard strange noises coming from the fireplace. Someone or something was scratching and rustling around inside the brick walls, just three feet away from me. It sounded like a very large animal. My heart began pulsating with fear as visions of vicious wolves and wild bears began to fill my head. Not that a bear could fit into the chimney, but I think my fever was making me a bit irrational.

The fireplace had no cover except a thin board, propped against the opening to keep out cold drafts. My eyes froze on the sparse piece of lumber; the only barrier between me and the unseen intruder. And as I watched in terror, the board moved. The unwelcome visitor was pushing against it, trying to get into the house! Suddenly, the tip of a sharp black claw poked through a small hole in the wood.

Trying to keep from screaming, I grabbed an armchair and wrestled it in front of the board. Then I snatched up a fire poker and sat poised, ready to fight whatever savage animal was about to break in and attack me. I waited there for an hour. The creature eventually gave up its pursuit and the clawing noises finally died down. But the rapid pace of my heart didn't slow for the rest of the day.

The animal in the fireplace turned out to be a raccoon. In fact, it was an entire family of raccoons that had decided to spend the winter in our chimney. Having grown up in suburbia, I was basically a wimp when it came to wildlife. I began to have nightmares of the raccoons pushing down the board, bursting into the house, and chasing me around the room with their razor sharp teeth. We tried many methods of extracting the raccoons, from setting traps to smoking them out, but like the fleas, nothing seemed to chase them away.

One night in the middle of another terrifying raccoon dream in which I lost three fingers and contracted rabies, I woke to the sound of a loud waterfall cascading through the kitchen. Eric and I rushed downstairs to find icy water spraying everywhere. The laundry room pipes had burst from the record-breaking cold.

Three hours later, after Eric's daring venture into the pitch-black, spider-infested crawl space under the house, the exploded pipe had stopped spraying water, the mess was cleaned up, and our washing machine was officially declared broken. As if we needed another trial.

In the space of a month, we'd been attacked by fleas, haunted by raccoons, plagued by sickness, stressed by financial challenges, and inconvenienced by a car that always seemed to die at the worse possible time. Now this? Though both of us had attempted to maintain a positive attitude, our spirits were seriously lagging.[1]

In those challenging first few months of marriage, God taught me an important lesson. Like many young women, I had always seen marriage as the time in my life when "everything would be perfect" and all my dreams would finally be fulfilled. I'd subconsciously been "postponing" joy and happiness until I was married to the man of my dreams, had three adorable children, and lived in a cute house with a rose garden and white picket fence.

But life isn't always predictable. Marriage isn't always perfect. And when we look to our spouses or our "fairy tale dreams" as the sources of our happiness and fulfillment, we'll usually be disappointed.

Only Jesus Christ can truly fulfill the deepest longings and desires of our feminine hearts. Before marriage, we often chase after temporary romantic flings, thinking that if we can only achieve the approval of the opposite sex, we'll be happy and fulfilled. After marriage, we often chase after a specific ideal in our spouses, thinking that if we can only get our husbands to be as romantic (and wealthy!) as Mr. Darcy from *Pride and Prejudice,* we'll be happy and fulfilled. Eric couldn't control the fleas or the weather or our finances. He couldn't sweep me away into a Jane Austen novel and rescue me from every discomfort I was facing. And as wonderful a husband as he was, he couldn't meet every romantic desire of my heart, 24 hours a day. So I had a choice to make.

I could either gripe, complain, nag, and nitpick until my ideal picture of married life was finally met (which might be never), or I could turn to the true Lover of my soul, Jesus Christ, and find my happiness and fulfillment in Him alone.

I chose the latter. Though it wasn't easy, I allowed Jesus Christ to be *enough*—to be everything I could ever want or need—even if none of my marriage dreams ever came true, even if we lived in that flea-infested house for the rest of our lives, and even if we never had enough money for Eric to buy me one flower.

An amazing thing happened when I began to seek my joy, peace, and fulfillment in my relationship with Christ instead of in my marriage "ideal." No longer was I looking to Eric (or to life circumstances) to meet needs that only my heavenly Prince could truly meet. And I found that I was able to treat Eric with a different attitude. Instead of always worrying about whether he was meeting *my* needs or fulfilling *my* romantic ideals, I was able to focus on serving him and giving to him.

The secret to a marriage thriving for a lifetime is *selflessness*. Nothing will kill a marriage faster than two people who are only concerned with meeting their own needs and desires. But nothing will cause the romance and beauty of a marriage to blossom like two people who put each other's needs and desires above their own.

Eric has truly been shaped into a heroic prince and husband. He grows more sensitive toward me and more romantic as the years go by. But it's not because I drop hints, criticize, or complain. It's because I allow my intimate relationship with Jesus Christ to fulfill the deepest desires of my heart rather than putting that pressure upon Eric's shoulders.

The reason that our love story thrives is because we make Jesus Christ our first love.

It's true that newlyweds can take unhealthy expectations into marriage. When we expect our spouses to meet needs that only Christ can meet, we will be disappointed. But here is the crucial truth we must realize: If we allow our marriages to be a beautiful outflow of a passionate relationship with Christ, *we will never be disillusioned.* A marriage that keeps Christ at the center only gets more amazing with time.

Richard and Sabina Wurmbrand (whom I introduced in chapter one) had the most romantic real-life love story I've ever heard of. But ironically their marriage was nothing like the "white picket fence" scenario that most of us dream about. Their life together was marked by intense persecution, torture, imprisonment, poverty, and over ten years of separation from each other. When Richard sat in the pastor's convention listening to the name of Christ being blasphemed, Sabina had a choice to make. She could either cling to her desire to keep her husband by her side and her family protected, or she could make Jesus Christ her highest priority. She chose to honor the name of Christ, even though it meant giving up everything in life that she held dear.

Richard was thrown into prison, and she spent ten years not knowing whether he was dead or alive. Was the beauty of their love story dimmed by such dismal circumstances? Just the opposite. After years of praying and agonizing for her husband, Sabina received a note, scrawled in Richard's unmistakable handwriting. He was only allowed to write a few words, which would be censored by prison guards. What could he say to his wife after years of separation and hardship? His words were more beautiful than any Jane Austen novel: *Time and distance quench a small love, but make a great love grow stronger.*

And it was proven true in their marriage. When Richard was finally released from prison, looking more like a skeleton than a man, he and Sabina had barely enough money to survive. When their anniversary came, neither had a penny to buy each other a gift, but Richard managed to obtain a small notebook in which he wrote every night—love letters to Sabina, the love of his life. After several months of bliss, Richard was betrayed by a fellow pastor who wanted to avoid prison. The guards stormed into their tiny attic apartment and prepared to haul Richard away once again.

"I won't go without a struggle," Richard told them quietly, "unless you allow me to embrace my wife."

Awkwardly the guards stepped back and watched as Richard and Sabina knelt together, sang a hymn, and prayed. The captain of the guard was so taken aback by such a tender scene that tears actually came to his eyes.

As Richard was being led away to prison for the second time he called out to Sabina, "Give my love to our son," he said, "and to the man who betrayed me."

After two more years of agonizing separation, Richard was ransomed and the couple escaped to America where they spent the rest of their lives laboring on behalf of the persecuted church. At the end of her life, Sabina called Richard to her side, expressed her great love for him, and asked him to forgive any shortcomings she had as his wife. Then she went home to meet her First Love. A short time later, Richard joined her in eternity.[2]

This couple had the undying passion and romance that all of us desire in a marriage, even though they had no earthly comforts, no marriage conferences, and no romantic getaways to the beach. In their ten years of separation, they weren't able to work on their communication skills or go on weekly "date nights." They never had a cute house with a rose garden and a white picket fence.

But they had the secret of lasting romance—a passionate love for Jesus Christ. Their marriage was the outflow of the greatest love story of all time—and as a result, it was a picture of heaven on earth.

Don't let the dismal predictions of well-meaning Christians dampen your expectations for how spectacular marriage can be. If you learn how to make Jesus Christ your first love, you will lay the foundation for the kind of marriage that grows stunningly beautiful with time—whether you live in a cute house with a white picket fence or in a filthy prison cell. Nothing can destroy the beauty of a romance built by God.

Living a set-apart life has affected every area of my daily existence: my relationships with others, my relationships with my family, how I relate to guys, and how I live out my daily life. It means sacrificing things that other Christians might consider acceptable, but there is no sweeter joy than resting in the knowledge and love of my beloved Prince, Jesus.

—Abby, 27

If you ever catch yourself "putting off" happiness until you finally get married or thinking that when you finally meet your spouse all of your dreams will be fulfilled, that's a sign that Christ hasn't fully captured your heart. If Jesus Christ isn't enough right now, then He won't be enough after marriage either. And you'll always be seeking fulfillment from the wrong things—setting your marriage up for disillusionment and tension.

If you want to prepare for a marriage that will last, cultivate your romance with Christ. Allow Him to captivate your heart and become your "all in all." And whether you ever get married or not, you will still experience the greatest love story of all time! (For additional practical insight on cultivating intimacy with Christ, I would recommend reading *Authentic Beauty*.)

Put Your Husband's Needs Above Your Own

During our wedding, Eric and I had a foot-washing ceremony. It was a statement that we intended to pour out our lives for each other just as Christ had poured out His life for us. While I washed Eric's feet, a song that I had written and recorded for Eric was played. It declared my desire to be his servant, to lay down my own dreams and plans and to pour my entire life into him. After the wedding, I discovered that some wives felt my statement of servanthood toward Eric was a little too extreme. In our book *The First 90 Days of Marriage*, I wrote about the criticism I received and what God has since taught me about what it really means to serve my husband:

> "I don't think you need to refer to yourself as Eric's servant," said one woman. "It sounds so demeaning. You aren't his slave, you know. You still have your own life." Other women agreed. "I think you are taking it too far," they told me. "Of course you want to help him and honor him, but a wife doesn't need to grovel at her husband's feet."
>
> I understood why these women were concerned about my desire to be Eric's servant. There is a common attitude among modern wives that says we must stand up for ourselves—to make sure our husbands never take us for granted, to make sure we are receiving just as much as we are giving. We fear that the moment we choose to give up the control position in our marriage, we have signed away our life and our identity. We think that when we humble ourselves to serve our husbands, we will lose our respect and dignity as a woman and become nothing but a doormat. But, as a great Christian woman once said, "Christ became even lower than a doormat." Christ did not scrape and grasp for His rights, His power, His control. He willingly sacrificed them in order to meet our greatest need. There is no greater lover than the One who stooped so low and sacrificed so much for the sake of His Beloved. Christ was not worried about what He would receive from us. He simply

gave—He willingly poured out His breath and blood because He loved us (Philippians 2:6).

This is how we are called to love our husbands. Not holding back—pouring ourselves out for our man with abandon. Not scraping for our own rights, not grasping for our own agenda, but humbling ourselves daily, seeking our spouse's good above our own.[3]

Many modern messages for women urge us to look out for ourselves. They say that we shouldn't become so busy meeting other people's needs that we forget to meet our own. But what does Christ say? "Take no thought for your life" (Matthew 6:25 kjv). And "whoever will be the greatest among you, let him be the servant of all" (see Mark 10:44).

Look at Christ's example when He was here on earth. He was so busy pouring out for others that He scarcely had time to sleep or eat. He was not self-focused or self-protective. And even though He was the Lord of heaven and earth, He wrapped a towel around His waist, bent His knee, and washed His disciples' feet. And He said, "If I then your Lord and Teacher, have washed your feet, you also ought to wash one another's feet. For I have given you an example that you should do as I have done to you" (John 13:14-15).

Early into my life with Eric, I found that reading marriage books often made me focus on the wrong things—always analyzing whether my needs were being met by my husband and becoming discontent with his shortcomings. God gently showed me that if I would simply apply His kingdom principle to my marriage—to follow the example of Christ and take no thought for my life—then all of my needs would be perfectly met. And it has been proven true over and over again. When I focus on pouring out for Eric and putting his needs above my own, I find that every emotional, spiritual, and physical need I have is supernaturally met by my heavenly King.

Be on guard against the "look out for yourself" message no matter how good it may sound. One woman I know was told by a Christian counselor that she had been working too hard serving her family and just needed to take some time to "pamper herself" (splurging on designer furniture, spending a wad on spa treatments, and pigging-out on chocolate). For some reason, I just can't imagine Christ taking time away from His ministry to "pamper Himself." The only personal area of His life that Jesus diligently protected was private times of prayer. If we ever become weary and encumbered with serving (like Martha in Luke 38), the answer is not going on a shopping spree or indulging in a box of chocolates. It is sitting at the feet of our King and letting Him renew and refresh us—body, soul, and spirit as Mary did.

When it comes to marriage, don't fight to protect yourself or constantly analyze whether your husband is meeting all your needs. The only thing you need to carefully protect is your daily time in Christ's presence. As you follow the example of Christ and pour out your life for your husband, you will discover a greater joy than any amount of self-focus could ever bring.

This is a habit that you can put into practice even before marriage. As you pray for your future husband, don't just focus on your own desires, but on how your prayers can help shape him into the mighty man God has called him to be. If you pray diligently for him every day and carry this practice into marriage, you will be amazed at how God molds and shapes him into the man your heart desires.

As a single woman, rather than putting life on hold until you get married, orient your life around joyfully serving others (as we will talk more about in the next chapter). As you practice becoming the servant of all, serving your husband will come naturally in marriage, and you will gain greater blessings than you could ever imagine.

> If you pour out yourself for the hungry and satisfy the desire of the afflicted, then shall your light rise in the darkness and your gloom shall be as the noonday. (Is 58) Here, I think, lies the answer to the barrenness of a single life, or of a life that might

otherwise be selfish or lonely. It is the answer, I have found, to depression as well. You yourself will be given light in exchange for pouring yourself out, you yourself will get guidance, the satisfaction of your longings, and strength when you pour yourself out; when you make the satisfaction of somebody else's desire your own concern.[4]

—ELISABETH ELLIOT

Sacred Claim

awakening femininity's heroic call

8

> For we are His workmanship, created in Christ Jesus for good works, which God prepared beforehand that we should walk in them (Ephesians 2:10).

🪶

I lack nothing. I have everything—everything I want in Christ. But that's not true for the world. There are millions and millions and millions of people who lack. They don't know those words about the Lord who feeds hungry people. Nobody ever told them that oppressed people could be freed. They live believing that corruption is the norm. They pay people back with what they've been paid—whether it's bad words or injustice or blows or beatings. That's what most of them know. For these people I have no excuse, for these you have no excuse. If you will not reach them with the love of God, if you will not tell them that there is a God who loves them—loves them enough to die to make them whole—who will? That's why He's allowed us to remain here. So that we can take His ministry to them. It's a

191

job that the angels longed to do. But He left it to you and me. Not just the responsibility—but the joy, the privilege of sharing good news.[1]

—JACKIE PULLENGER

A Christian publisher once told me, "You shouldn't always write about missionary Christians like Gladys Aylward and Amy Carmichael. Why don't you share about some normal, everyday Christians who live in the suburbs and work for IBM? Those kinds of Christians are just as important as the ones who go to the mission field. Don't just focus on Christians who had a 'special calling' to go and change the world."

Well, sorry to be so blunt, but most "normal, everyday" Christians in the Western world are living pleasure-seeking, self-absorbed lives. Just think about it. Are we, as the majority of American Christians, pouring ourselves out for the lost and the least, or are we lying on our couches, eating pizza, and watching reality TV? Millions of hurting, destitute, hopeless people are crying out for someone to help them. But sadly, we are frighteningly similar to the wealthy Christians during the Holocaust who sat comfortably in church singing hymns at the tops of their lungs to drown out the anguished cries of the thousands of Jews who passed by in cattle cars on their way to death camps. We, like those Christians in Germany, are turning a deaf ear to the cries of the desperate.

No matter what my publisher friend says, we don't need more of that kind of Christian. We need more Gladys Aylwards, Amy Carmichaels, and Jackie Pullengers. Those women didn't have a "special" calling on their lives. Rather, they were among the few who actually recognized and obeyed the sacred call that Christ has placed upon *every single man or woman* who claims to know Him.

When the Son of Man comes in His glory, and all the holy angels with Him, then He will sit on the throne of His glory. All the nations will be gathered before Him, and He will separate them one from another, as a shepherd divides his sheep from the goats. And He will set the sheep on His right hand, but the goats on the left.

Then the King will say to those on His right hand, "Come, you blessed of My Father, inherit the kingdom prepared for you from the foundation of the world: for I was hungry and you gave Me food; I was thirsty and you gave Me drink; I was a stranger and you took Me in; I was naked and you clothed Me; I was sick and you visited Me; I was in prison and you came to Me." Then the righteous will answer Him, saying, "Lord, when did we see You hungry and feed You, or thirsty and give You drink? When did we see You a stranger and take You in, or naked and clothe You? Or when did we see You sick, or in prison, and come to You?"

And the King will answer and say to them, "Assuredly, I say to you, inasmuch as you did it to one of the least of these My brethren, you did it to Me."

Then He will also say to those on the left hand, "Depart from Me, you cursed, into the everlasting fire prepared for the devil and his angels: for I was hungry and you gave Me no food; I was thirsty and you gave Me no drink; I was a stranger and you did not take Me in, naked and you did not clothe Me, sick and in prison and you did not visit Me." Then they also will answer Him, saying, "Lord, when did we see You hungry or thirsty or a stranger or naked or sick or in prison, and did not minister to You?" Then He will answer them, saying, "Assuredly, I say to you, inasmuch as you did not do it to one of the least of these, you did not do it to Me." And these will go away into everlasting punishment, but the righteous into eternal life (Matthew 25:31-46).

As we discussed earlier in this book, modern Christianity goes out of its way to convince us that the Christian life is all about *us*. The majority of today's Bible studies, sermons, and Christian books causes us to focus on what *we* are feeling, what *we* are needing, and what *we* are struggling with. Here is the publisher's description of that popular women's book *Captivating.* "The message of *Captivating* is this: Your heart matters more than anything else in all creation." And what is meant by the term "your heart"? According to the author of the book, "The heart is who we are. The real self. Me. My heart is me. The real me. Your heart is you."[2]

So in other words, *you* matter more than anything else in all creation.

Really?

Do *you* matter more than the 143 million orphans around the world, starving, scared, abandoned, and alone? Do *you* matter more than the millions of Latin American street children who hide in alleys and old buildings to escape the "death squads" of corrupt policemen who hunt them down for sport? Do *you* matter more than the millions of elementary school-aged girls kept as slave prostitutes in South America? Do *you* matter more than millions of starving kids who live in dumps and eat buzzard soup or dead dogs to survive? Do *you* matter more than the countless African boys who have seen their parents killed and been forced to rape or kill to stay alive? Do *you* matter more than the scores of six-year-old African girls who have been repeatedly brutalized and raped by HIV-infected men?

While American Christians are preoccupied with healing their own inner wounds, being set free to be their true selves, and fighting to be noticed and appreciated for their own unique qualities, staggering numbers of people around the world are living in such misery, squalor, and pain that we cannot even imagine.

Earlier this year, the movie *Amazing Grace* acquainted us with the heroic life of William Wilberforce as he courageously fought to put an end to the slave trade. Those who saw the movie felt elated when he finally succeeded. And many of us wished for the opportunity to do something so noble on behalf of suffering humanity.

But here is a startling fact. Though Wilberforce succeeded in his specific battle for slaves, the worldwide problem of slavery has not ended. In fact, there are 27 million slaves in the world today, which is *higher* than in the days of William Wilberforce or at any other time in history.[3]

We do not live in a world of peace and harmony. There are urgent battles for injustice waiting to be fought. There are countless human lives desperately waiting to be rescued. There are millions of precious children facing unspeakable suffering.

And like Jackie Pullenger said, if Christ's set-apart ones do not act as His hands and feet to them…who will?

Most of us would be horrified at the thought of ignoring a cattle car of screaming Jews as they were hauled away to their deaths. But we do it every single day when we turn a deaf ear and a blind eye to the millions of destitute and dying who urgently need our help. We do it when we spend all our living on self-indulgent pleasures instead of on rescuing abandoned children. We do it when we go on luxury cruises instead of outreaches to the poor. We do it when we have movie marathons instead of prayer vigils for the oppressed. We do it every time we make our own comforts and happiness the highest priority. We do it whenever we fall for the idea that *we* are the most important people in all creation.

In 1860 as the Salvation Army became an advocate for the poor and impoverished in England, Catherine Booth wrote a challenge to the self-absorbed Christian women of her country. "It will be a happy day for England when Christian ladies transfer their attention from poodles and terriers to destitute and starving children."[4]

Catherine told them in no uncertain terms that they were addicted to pleasure—to eating, drinking, dressing, riding, and sightseeing and far too absorbed with self to truly serve God.

These days, Christian women have the same problem. It might not be poodles and terriers that have our attention, but it is certainly not destitute and dying children. A popular Christian "Biblezine" for women proclaims, "Want a new you in the New Year? Here's your New Testament! Tailoring transforming truth into a women's magazine format, this take-anywhere 'Biblezine' brims with practical tips for fitting your life to your faith! Easy-reading text with articles on worship, beauty, men, health, career, relationships, and more!" [5]

Somehow even the Bible has become all about *us*. In a diabolical twist, the New Testament has morphed into being all about *our* interests, such as beauty, men, health, career, and relationships (oh yes, worship was in the list too, wasn't it?), rather than serving, loving, giving, and laboring for the kingdom of God. Ian Thomas wrote:

> It is startling to discover that even God may be used as an excuse for worshipping yourself, demonstrating again the satanic genius for distorting truth and deceiving man—for it was to this temptation that Adam and Eve fell in the Garden! [6]

And it is to that temptation that modern Christian womanhood has fallen as well. We are so self-absorbed that even our so-called worship of Christ has been twisted into worshipping ourselves, focusing on ourselves, and seeking after our own pleasures.

Browsing in the women's section of the Christian bookstore, you'll see a myriad of titles that encourage you to "discover your intrinsic value" or get "comfortable in your own skin," but very few that echo the words of Paul:

> Let nothing be done through selfish ambition or conceit, but in lowliness of mind let each esteem others better than himself. Let this mind be in you which was also in Christ Jesus, who, being in the form of God, did not consider it robbery to be equal with God, but made Himself of no reputation, taking the form of a bondservant (Philippians 2:3,5-7).

Or the words of James:

> Pure and undefiled religion before God and the Father is this: to visit orphans and widows in their trouble, and to keep oneself unspotted from the world (James 1:27).

Or the words of Christ:

> If anyone desires to come after Me, let him deny himself, and
> take up his cross daily, and follow Me. For whoever desires to
> save his life will lose it, but whoever loses his life for My sake
> will save it (Luke 9:23-24).

Our hearts are *not* the most important things in the world.

The Down syndrome boy in Mexico City who sleeps on the street and begs for food is the most important thing in the world. The nine-year-old girl whose virginity is auctioned off to a roomful of despicable perverts is the most important thing in the world. The impoverished prostitute who lives in the gutter and sells her body for a few coins a day is the most important thing in the world. The African boy-soldier who is forced to become a killing machine at the age of ten is the most important thing in the world.

Scripture says that God is no respecter of persons. In other words, He does not withhold the blessings of His kingdom based on our race, sex, or background (see Galatians 3:28). All of us are valuable and equal in His sight. However, there are some people who have His special favor. There are some who are extra close to His heart. They are the poor, the lame, the weak, and the outcast. The ones whom the world treats as scum are the ones we are called to treat as royalty.

> When you give a dinner or a supper, do not ask your friends,
> your brothers, your relatives, nor rich neighbors, lest they also
> invite you back, and you be repaid. But when you give a feast,
> invite the poor, the maimed, the lame, the blind. And you will
> be blessed because they cannot repay you; for you shall be
> repaid at the resurrection of the just (Luke 14:12-14).

He raises the poor from the dust and lifts the beggar from the ash heap to set them among princes and make them inherit the throne of glory (1 Samuel 2:8).

I delivered the poor that cried, and the fatherless, and him that had none to help him. The blessing of him that was ready to perish came upon me: and I caused the widow's heart to sing for joy. I put on righteousness, and it clothed me: my judgment was as a robe and a diadem. I was eyes to the blind, and feet was I to the lame. I was a father to the poor: and the cause which I knew not I searched out. And I broke the jaws of the wicked, and plucked the spoil out of his teeth (Job 29:12-17).

This is the pattern of the Gospel. To do as Christ did. To seek and save the lost.

Our hearts are valuable to Christ, yes. He loved us so intensely that He gave up His very life to rescue us and set us free. But *why* does He set us free? *Why* does He make us whole? *Why* does He protect us, heal us, bless us, and provide for us? *Why* does He make us into strong, valiant, virtuous women? So that we can spend our lives living in selfish pleasure, comfort, and ease? So that we can selfishly soak up the benefits and blessings of Christ while the rest of the world is dying?

Jesus said, "As the Father has sent Me, I also send you" (John 20:21). He sets us free so that we can become like Him. So that we can be for others as He was for us—a poured-out living sacrifice that places others' needs above our own. So that our lives can be a living, breathing testimony of the love that triumphs over all. As it says in Galatians, "For you, brethren, have been called to liberty; only do not use liberty as an opportunity for the flesh, but through love serve one another. For all the law is fulfilled in one word, even in this: you shall love your neighbor as yourself" (Galatians 5:13-14).

When Christ spoke to the teacher of the law who asked Him what he must do to be saved, He gave a vivid picture of what it means to love our neighbor as ourselves:

> And behold, a certain lawyer stood up and tested Him, saying, "Teacher, what shall I do to inherit eternal life?"
>
> He said to him, "What is written in the law? What is your reading of it?"
>
> So he answered and said, "You shall love the LORD your God with all your heart, with all your soul, with all your strength, and with all your mind and your neighbor as yourself."
>
> And He said to him, "You have answered rightly; do this and you will live."
>
> But he, wanting to justify himself, said to Jesus, "And who is my neighbor?"
>
> Then Jesus answered and said: "A certain man went down from Jerusalem to Jericho, and fell among thieves, who stripped him of his clothing, wounded him, and departed, leaving him half dead. Now by chance a certain priest came down that road. And when he saw him, he passed by on the other side. Likewise a Levite, when he arrived at the place, came and looked, and passed by on the other side. But a certain Samaritan, as he journeyed, came where he was. And when he saw him, he had compassion. So he went to him and bandaged his wounds, pouring on oil and wine; and he set him on his own animal, brought him to an inn, and took care of him. On the next day, when he departed, he took out two denarii, gave them to the innkeeper, and said to him, 'Take care of him; and whatever more you spend, when I come again, I will repay you.' So which of these three do you think was neighbor to him who fell among the thieves?"

And he said, "He who showed mercy on him."

Then Jesus said to him, "Go and do likewise" (Luke 10: 25-37).

Millions cry out for someone to bind their wounds, feed them, clothe them, and proclaim the unmatched hope of Christ to them. Are we running to their aid, or are we passing by on the other side of the street?

> Jesus never came and said, "I love you." He didn't say it—He showed it. He didn't just bless us—He died for us. He wept for us. He gave up His life for you, and now He is asking you to share everything He has given you with others.[7]
>
> —JACKIE PULLENGER

> By this we know love, because He laid down His life for us. And we also ought to lay down our lives for the brethren. But whoever has this world's goods, and sees his brother in need, and shuts up his heart from him, how does the love of God abide in him? My little children, let us not love in word or in tongue, but in deed and in truth (1 John 3:16-18).

The Claim

Taking communion is a statement of our covenant with Christ. When we "eat of His body" and "drink of His blood," we gain access to everything He purchased for us on the cross: forgiveness, freedom, hope, healing, and eternal life. In essence, we each have a sacred claim to His kingdom. We each have the "right" to call upon Him for our every need. Through His covenant with us, He has bound Himself to us.

> Then Jesus said to them, "Most assuredly, I say to you, unless you eat the flesh of the Son of Man and drink His blood, you have no life in you. Whoever eats My flesh and drinks My blood has eternal life, and I will raise him up at the last day. For My flesh is

food indeed, and My blood is drink indeed. He who eats My flesh and drinks My blood abides in Me, and I in him. As the living Father sent Me, and I live because of the Father, so he who feeds on Me will live because of Me" (John 6:53-57).

We have a claim to all that Christ offers. And in the last chapter on fortification, we talked about what it means to live in that glorious reality.

But there is another side to our covenant with Him. Just as we have a claim upon Him, *Jesus Christ has a claim upon us.* Remember Leonard Ravenhill's definition of being a Christian? "You have no time of your own, no money of your own. Christ must become your complete Master."[8]

When we partake of holy communion, we are not just remembering what Christ did for us. We are stating to our Master that through this covenant, our bodies and blood are His to spend as He chooses. His body and blood for us. *Our body and blood for Him.*

Paul says, "Do you not know that your bodies are members of Christ?" (1 Corinthians 6:15). We are the body of Christ. We are His hands and feet. What do Christ's hands and feet do? They bind wounds. They offer forgiveness. They set captives free. They heal the sick. They minister to children. They seek out the sinner. They drive out evil from the temple of God. They walk the road to Calvary. And they are pierced through that we might be saved.

If you have chosen the set-apart path of a woman who fears the Lord, your life is not your own. The Spirit of Christ has a claim upon you. You have a call upon your life. You have a job to do. He has called you to minister His love to those in need. This sacred claim is the highest privilege we could ever receive. We can never repay what Christ did for us on the cross. But because He has made us His hands and feet to this world, we have the incredible opportunity to give to others the very same astounding, transforming love that He gave to us.

Our act of worship is to offer our bodies to Him as living sacrifices. This is not just sitting in our comfortable church buildings and singing about how much we love Him. It is demonstrating our love for Christ by practically giving it to those who desperately need it.

> If a brother or sister is naked and destitute of daily food, and one of you says to them, "Depart in peace, be warmed and filled," but you do not give them the things which are needed for the body, what does it profit? Thus also faith by itself, if it does not have works, is dead (James 2:15-17).

The world is absolutely flooded with those who are destitute of daily food and clothes. About 25,000 people die every day of hunger or hunger-related causes, according to the United Nations. That's one person every three and a half seconds.[9] In Latin America and Africa, countless children are addicted to inhalants as a means of deadening their senses to their bodies' desperate cries for food. In Liberia thousands of pregnant women and young children pound rocks all day long on the side of a mountain and in the hot sun just to get one bowl of watery rice.

These people have a claim on your life. They have a claim on my life. They are a priority to Christ and therefore must become a priority to us. If we are so preoccupied with self that we will not show the practical, life-changing, hope-giving love of Christ to them, our faith is dead.

> And though I have the gift of prophecy, and understand all mysteries and all knowledge, and though I have all faith, so that I could remove mountains, but have not love, I am nothing (1 Corinthians 13:2).

Just because we might live in the suburbs and don't see homeless children begging on the streets every day does not give us an excuse to ignore the cries of the poor. Jesus went to *seek* and save the lost. He did not stay among the wealthy and important. He went out of His way to find those in need. And He calls us to follow in His steps.

What I eat, what I wear, how I spend my time, how I spend money, and what I do for fun may not seem like such big deals to most people, but it's in learning to honor God with all these little, tiny, everyday details that I can truly live a life "set apart" and glorifying to Him! While God cares about the big milestones, it's the daily, little "nitty-gritty" that I am constantly learning to place under His control. "He that is faithful in that which is least is faithful also in much" (Luke 16:10 KJV). Being set apart for God is not just another part of life for me—it's a whole paradigm shift. It's a lifestyle!

—Melody, 32

The Direction of Your Life

As set-apart young women, we must seriously consider the kinds of lives Christ has called us to live.

The publisher I mentioned earlier seems to think that Christianity is made up of comfortable, well-off, self-indulgent individuals who live primarily for their own pleasures and go on short-term mission trips every couple of years to ease their consciences.

But *true* Christianity is made up of radically abandoned, poured-out, servant-hearted individuals who give their entire lives to build the kingdom to God. Women like Amy Carmichael, Jackie Pullenger, and Gladys Aylward didn't merely lay down their rights to live comfortable, upper-middle class lives. They laid down *every right* they possessed for the kingdom and glory of God. They willingly sacrificed their rights to be married, their rights to live near their families and friends, their rights to be recognized and appreciated, and their rights to financial security—all for the supreme privilege of being Christ's hands and feet to a dying world.

As a 20-year-old woman, Jackie Pullenger walked through the drug-infested squalor of the Walled City in Hong Kong, seeing hopeless old men addicted to opium, desperate young gang members who used violence to gain respect, and destitute women who sold their bodies all day and night to buy one bowl of rice, and her heart broke for them. She prayed, "It would be worth my whole life if I could reach just one for You, Lord."[10]

Can we say those very same words—and mean them? It's a question that challenges me at the deepest level. Would I be willing to give up everything I hold dear to save that one Down syndrome boy on the streets of Mexico City or that one child prostitute in Brazil? Would I lay down my own life to set free just one child soldier in Africa?

God might not call every one of us to the Walled City of Hong Kong like Jackie Pullenger or the temples of India like Amy Carmichael. And He doesn't ask us all to remain single for our entire life to serve His kingdom. It is true that He has unique roles for each of us to play in His great drama and that each of us are called to different things.

But *not one of us* is "called" to live the self-indulgent, pleasure-seeking, comfort-craving life of the typical American Christian. If you think that God has called you to merely live in a nice house with a well-paying job and be part of a Bible study group, then you aren't very familiar with what His Word says. It's not that living in a nice house, having a well-paying job, or joining a Bible study is wrong. But those things are not the essence of the Christian life.

There is a sacred claim upon each of our lives that is not to be ignored. Christ makes us whole so that we can be *poured out* for Him. Not once a year. Not even two or three times a week. He has called us to be a living sacrifice—to live *a lifestyle* of serving and sacrifice for His kingdom.

Even raising children can be used as an excuse to ignore the sacred claims on our lives. I cannot even count the number of Christian women I have seen who think that their only calling is to raise their own kids. They feel completely justified in ignoring the needs of a dying world because they are too busy pushing strollers through the mall and taking their children to the park. It's true that God puts great value on a woman bringing up children. Raising kids and guiding the home is a high priority in His kingdom.

But it is not the *only* priority. In fact, raising children is just *one* of the heroic things that the Proverbs 31 woman does. She also reaches out to the poor and stretches out her hands to the needy. She diligently sows and reaps for the kingdom of God. The virtuous woman in 1 Timothy is similar. Bringing up children is *one* of her qualities. But she also excels in good works, lodging strangers, washing the saints' feet, and relieving the afflicted. (And as we discussed earlier, she accomplishes all this not by striving and effort, but by the supernaturally enabling grace of God—accessed and realized through fervent prayer and continual yielding to Him.)

Elizabeth Fry had 11 children and Catherine Booth had eight. They were amazing mothers and managers of their homes. And yet they radically poured out their lives for the oppressed and needy, to the point that entire continents were radically altered and millions came into God's kingdom because of their sacrifices.

Beware of downplaying the sacred claim that God has upon your life under the banner of being "called" to suburbia or to simply be a mom. There is nothing wrong with suburbia or with focusing a large amount of your time on raising children, especially while your children are young. But be sure you don't use those things as an excuse to ignore the greater call upon your life—pouring out with radical abandon for the lost, dying, needy, and oppressed.

Answering the Call

Jackie Pullenger once said that when you hear of someone in a desperate situation, you cannot assume that someone else is going to take care of it. You need to act as if you are the only one who knows of the need, and that God has specially chosen you to meet it.[11] (And if it is impossible for you to meet the need practically, it is never impossible for you to meet the need spiritually by laboring for that person or people in fervent prayer.)

Earlier this year, God challenged me on this very point. On a Friday afternoon in April, Eric and I walked into an adoption agency that specialized in Chinese and Korean adoptions. It was just supposed to be an "information gathering" step. We had recently been challenged by Christ's Spirit to look for ways in which we could practically become His hands and feet to needy children around the world, and we wanted to learn more about orphaned children in need of loving homes. We weren't necessarily thinking about adopting a child anytime soon, but we wanted to at least meet with an agency and find out what kind of need there was and what the process was like.

We had no idea how that meeting would change our lives. We were told that there was quite a line-up of families waiting to adopt a healthy child and the wait was usually about two years. But there were many "special needs" children who were currently waiting and in desperate need of homes. Most families passed over these children because they didn't want to deal with the physical issues that came with them.

"What do you mean by 'special needs'?" I questioned.

"Well, for example, we have a newborn baby girl with no fingers and deformed feet."

The agency worker pulled out a manila folder and slid a photo across the table. It was a picture of two baby hands—missing all the fingers except thumbs. As I stared at the tiny misshapen hands, I felt a strange tug upon my heart. I hadn't even seen the child's face, and already I was gripped with an intense concern for her life.

"We've had several families look at her file," we were told. "But so far no one has wanted to adopt her."

"What happens if no one adopts her?" I asked.

"She'll grow up in an institution," was the blunt answer.

As Eric and I drove home, all we could think about was the little girl with no fingers. Inexplicably, we both started to cry. We decided to pray for her. Eric began, and through a flood of emotion, said the only thing that came to his mind, the words of Psalm 68:5: "A father of the fatherless, a defender of widows, is God in His holy habitation. God sets the solitary in families."

We felt as if the presence of God was in the car with us as we asked Him for His heart for this precious orphaned child. When we arrived home, an email was waiting for us from someone who had no idea that we were visiting an adoption agency or looking into helping orphans. She wrote, "I was praying this morning, and just felt God wanted me to share this verse with you: *A father of the fatherless, a defender of widows, is God in His holy habitation. God sets the solitary in families.*"

Needless to say, God had our attention! We spent the rest of that day and evening asking God how He wanted us to respond. We knew of a child who desperately needed a home. She'd been rejected by her parents because of her deformities. She'd been passed over by adoptive families for the same reason. But God had not rejected her. He had not forgotten her. Somehow, all the way from the other side of the world, He had placed those tiny hands in front of us. And like Jackie Pullenger said, we couldn't just assume that someone else would meet her need. What if we were the ones God had chosen to be His hands and feet to her?

That night, we went online and looked at a photo of the little girl's face. As I studied her picture, I prayed, "God, if You desire this child to be our daughter, then flood us with an overwhelming love for her even now."

When I woke up the next morning, I had no doubt in my mind. This baby was to be our child. Even though I had only seen one grainy photo, I felt my heart would explode with overwhelming love and concern for her—and I knew that it was something God had done within me. Eric was in full agreement that this was exactly what God was doing—as unexpected and unplanned as it was.

We had no idea where the money for the adoption would come from. We had no idea where we would even find the time to go about the process. But we knew that this child had a sacred claim upon us, and that God would back us up with each step of obedience to Him. And He didn't let us down.

Three months later, Harper Grace Ludy arrived home. The cost of her adoption was miraculously provided for. The process was supernaturally governed. And the promise of Isaiah 58, that when we "bring the poor that are cast out into our house, our light will break forth as the morning," has been proven true in our lives. Many people say, "Oh, she is so blessed that you took her in!" But we feel that the opposite is true. *We* are the ones receiving the blessing. And I cannot imagine life without her. Christ said, "Whoever receives one little child like this in My name receives Me" (Matthew 18:5).

Every day, when I look into my daughter's eyes, I see Christ looking back at me.

Where to Begin

When you think about the countless millions of needy people in the world, it can be overwhelming to think about what you can possibly do to make a dent. But as you pray about what kind of "poured-out" life God has called you to, don't get caught up in a "ten-year plan" for eliminating world hunger. Rather, ask God to open your eyes to the ones you are called to reach *right now.* Before Eric and I walked into the adoption agency, we were daunted by the thought of helping the millions of orphans in need. We didn't even know where to start. But as we asked God to show us which children had a sacred claim upon us, He opened our eyes to the little girl with no fingers. We knew that in order to reach the 143 million orphans around the world, we had to start with one. And He faithfully showed us which one we were to reach first. We have a strong sense that Harper is only the first of *many* orphans we are called to demonstrate Christ's love to, but we are relying on God's Spirit to open our eyes to each step of obedience we are to take along the way.

No matter where you live or what your circumstances are, you can begin to fulfill the sacred claim upon your life. There are lonely, hungry, and oppressed people in every town, school, and neighborhood. Ask Christ's Spirit to open your eyes to see them. Ask Him to grant you the boldness and selflessness needed to showcase His love to them. And get ready to experience the greatest joy you could ever imagine.

Some Practical Suggestions

Thousands in our generation are in search of "spiritual employment"—looking for ways to become Christ's hands and feet to a dying world. If you are longing to make a difference, I'd encourage you to visit www.braveheartedgospel.com where you can learn about opportunities to become part of an international rescue mission for orphans and enslaved children around the world.

Sacred Ceremony

joining the fellowship of set-apart femininity

This sacred work demands, not lukewarm, selfish, slack souls, but hearts more finely tempered than steel, wills purer and harder than the diamond.

—PERE HENRI LOUIS DIDON

May I not hope that the God who came in power to eleven defeated men on the day of Pentecost, and by their means turned the world upside down, will come in power in this dark generation and do again His mighty works?[1]

—DR. WILLIAM EDWIN SANGSTER

Holy Kinship

When Amy Carmichael began her work of rescuing children from temple prostitution in India, she longed for other women to join her—women who were "wholly devoted to Christ and separate in spirit from the world." Not surprisingly, women like this were hard to find, and Amy labored alone for many years. But eventually, God drew seven

211

young women to join her in fulfilling the sacred claim of the set-apart life. Amy wrote, "These girls were seeking to live a life of unreserved devotion, a life without fences." They formed a sacred fellowship, covenanting together to live in unity, prayer, and absolute devotion to Jesus Christ. Their purpose was "to go all lengths with their Lord."

Together, these seven women formed a fellowship called "The Sisters of the Common Life." On March 18, 1916, they went into the forest for a time of prayer and consecration. Together, they drafted a written confession, signed it solemnly before God and each other, and committed to live by its principles. It was as follows:

- My Vow—Whatsoever Thou sayest unto me, by Thy grace I will do it
- My Constraint—Thy love, O Christ, my Lord
- My Confidence—Thou art able to keep that which I have committed unto Thee
- My Joy—To do Thy will, O God
- My Discipline—That which I would not choose, but which Thy love appoints
- My Prayer—Conform my will to Thine
- My Motto—Love to live: Live to love
- My Portion—The Lord is the portion of mine inheritance

This creed carried these young women through many years of intensive pouring-out on behalf of Christ. When trials came, when the enemy attempted to thwart and discourage, and when the allurements of the world beckoned, these sisters remembered the sacred ceremony that had bonded them together and held fast to the creed they each had sworn their lives to uphold.[2]

Nearly two centuries earlier in Scotland, a similar creed was signed by a group of Christ followers who covenanted together to preserve the immutability of Scripture. In a time when the religion of Rome had overshadowed the entire country and usurped the authority of the Word of God, these Covenanters signed a solemn vow to stand against all that would seek to undermine the purity of the Christian faith. "We detest and refuse the usurped authority of that Roman Antichrist upon the Scriptures of God, upon the civil magistrates and upon the conscience of men," the creed stated. All who signed it pledged to promote evangelical doctrine and discipline in scriptural purity. So sacred was this written confession to its adherents that many of the names written on it were signed in blood. It was a statement that they were willing to give their very lives to protect that which was precious to Christ.[3]

It may not seem like it at first glance, but you and I live in a perilous time, not unlike that of the Covenanters. In our generation, the purity of the Gospel is at stake, the bride of Christ is polluted and defiled by the world's attractions, and the Word of God is belittled by those who profess to bear His name. A new generation of Covenanters and Sisters of the Common Life is desperately needed.

As I have placed my finger on the pulse of today's Christian young women, I have observed the formation of two camps. The first camp is the larger and more popular one. It includes girls like Maria, who simply want to blend a dose of Christianity into their self-indulgent, pleasure-seeking, sin-ruled lives. The girls in this camp might read Christian books, sing Christian songs, and live according to Christian morals, but they are unwilling to "go to all lengths with their Lord" like the Sisters of the Common Life. They may possess a measure of feminine beauty, but it is a hollow, fleeting beauty of their own making. When it comes down to the wire, they will protect self rather than taking up the cross of Jesus Christ. As I have said throughout this book, this dying world does not need more of that kind of Christian young woman, and heaven is certainly not impressed with such mediocrity.

If you have made it this far in reading this book, you are likely leaning toward the second camp. Those in this camp are women like Jia and Jackie, women who are so radically abandoned to their precious

Lord and Master that the world holds no appeal and self-comfort is the very least of their concerns. They possess a stunning beauty that is not of this world—it is the spectacular radiance of Jesus Christ cascading through their beings. Self has been denied, and complete access has been granted to the Spirit of God to overtake their entire existence. There are not many who are willing to take the Christian life this seriously. But those who join this camp cause heaven to applaud and hell to tremble.

If you feel a pressure upon your soul to become a part of this second camp, this set-apart fellowship of Christ-ruled young women, then I invite you to enter into a scared ceremony—to join with me and with the other young women who are willing to "go to all lengths with their Lord" in boldly declaring our commitment to protect what is precious to Christ by life or by death. This sacred ceremony is not to be entered into lightly. The Covenanters in Scotland signed their confession of faith with their own blood. The Sisters of the Common Life left home, comfort, family, and friends and placed themselves in daily peril for the sake of their solemn creed. So if you are in—be *all* in.

Remember that in signing the following confession, you aren't merely committing to the principles expressed in this book, but you are joining the ranks of set-apart women throughout history—Vibia Perpetua, Catherine Booth, Gladys Aylward, Amy Carmichael, Elizabeth Fry, Sabina Wurmbrand, Jackie Pullenger, and countless more.

> Since we are surrounded by so great a cloud of witnesses, let us lay aside every weight, and the sin which so easily ensnares us, and let us run with endurance the race that is set before us (Hebrews 12:1).

You may be physically alone when you participate in this sacred ceremony, but you are not spiritually alone. Even if there are no other young women in your life who can join with you as you enter this holy fellowship, remember that there are countless women throughout history who are cheering you on. And remember that there is a remnant of young women in your very generation who are making this same confession before God.

Even more importantly, Jesus Christ, the Author and Finisher of your faith is standing beside you, joyfully welcoming you to join the privileged few who are called to be His true ambassadors of light in a dark and perverse generation.

I would encourage you to set aside a period of time when you can truly be alone with Him; where no interruptions will distract you. You may even want to darken the room, light candles, and play worshipful music or in some other creative way make an atmosphere that is fitting for a sacred ceremony in the presence of God. I would also encourage you to consider taking communion as part of this ceremony. You don't have to be in church to "drink of Christ's body and eat of His blood." It can be a beautiful private form of declaring your covenant relationship with Jesus Christ: His body and blood for you, your body and blood for Him. Allow His Spirit to lead you in when and how to enter into this ceremony. There is no formula for it. It is meant to be a time of intimacy between you and your King.

The following creed proclaims the commitments of a set-apart woman. As the Spirit of God leads you, read each line prayerfully and sign this confession when you are ready to give your life to protect this covenant. You might consider printing and framing a copy of this creed, placing it somewhere you will always be reminded of the sacred call upon your life. (You can download a printable version of this creed at www.setapartgirl.com.) My hope and prayer is that as you begin this sacred ceremony, your spirit will echo the words of David Brainerd.

> I enjoyed great sweetness in communion with my dear Savior. I think I never in my life felt such an entire weaneedness from this world and so much resigned to God in everything. Oh, that I may always live to God!

The Creed of the Set-Apart Young Woman

As a young woman submitted to the ruling grace of Jesus Christ, I acknowledge that my life is not my own. I have been purchased by the spilling of my Messiah's blood. I surrender this earthly feminine vessel unto my Lord and proclaim that He may do with my life as He sees fit in order to establish His kingdom here on earth, make ready His bride, and bring about His glory.

The Sacred Intent of Femininity

I acknowledge the sacred intent of set-apart femininity. I acknowledge that my life is to be spent wholly on the establishment of Christ's kingdom and glory. I have been asked by the Most High God to be the bearer of His holy name, the house of His holy presence, and a demonstration of a clear, undiluted, and unmarred picture of His kingly beauty for all the people of this earth to see. I acknowledge this sacred intent and commit, by the enabling power of the Holy Spirit, to seek the fulfillment of this high calling.

The Sacred Design of Femininity

I acknowledge the sacred design of set-apart femininity. I understand that in and of myself, I possess no true beauty or piety, but that in covenant exchange with the Almighty, I have yielded my body unto Jesus and He desires to adorn me with His spectacular, heavenly beauty. I will no longer allow the voice of my selfish, sinful side to rule my actions and daily decisions; rather, I will submit to the voice of God's Spirit within, leaning on His enabling grace to live the radiant, victorious, supernatural existence that I could never achieve in my own strength. May He instruct me, correct me, train me, and tenderly shepherd me in the hallowed art of being set apart for His pleasure and glory. I acknowledge this sacred design and commit, by the enabling power of the Holy Spirit, to seek the fulfillment of this high calling.

The Sacred Priority of Femininity

I acknowledge the sacred priority of set-apart femininity. I understand that I am made to love intimately and be loved intimately. But I choose to not pervert this innate need by seeking its fulfillment from men, but rather, that I would find this hunger satisfied in the intimate embrace of Jesus Christ. I acknowledge Jesus as more than my precious Savior, more than my Lord and Master, more than my King and Commander—I acknowledge Him as my Prince and Bridegroom, my dearest heart-friend. I claim that my life, my faith, my hope, and my love spring forth from this wellspring, this reality. And whereas God may choose to give me an earthly groom, a mere man can never and must never replace the position Christ holds within my heart. I acknowledge this sacred priority and commit, by the enabling power of the Holy Spirit, to seek the fulfillment of this high calling.

The Sacred Decorum of Femininity

I acknowledge the sacred decorum of set-apart femininity. I understand that my body is the temple of the Most High God, not to be tainted or defiled by what is unclean. I choose this day to agree with God and to never willfully profane His truth by attempting to make it fit my self-agenda. By God's enabling grace, I will love the things that God loves and hate the things that God hates. I will not love the world or the things in the world, but will give my thoughts, time, energy, and attention to the sacred things of His kingdom rather than the profane things of pop culture. I acknowledge this sacred decorum and commit, by the enabling power of the Holy Spirit, to seek the fulfillment of this high calling.

The Sacred Mystique of Femininity

I acknowledge the sacred mystique of set-apart femininity. I realize that there are dimensions of the feminine nature intended to be kept curtained and hidden from all but Christ and my future spouse in the context of marriage. I understand that by maintaining the beautiful mystery of the "hidden person of the heart," I am demonstrating the beautiful mystery of the Gospel. I choose to allow the Almighty to hide me, quiet me, and jealously guard me in accordance with His sacred sense of dignity and mystery. I acknowledge this sacred mystique and commit, by the enabling power of the Holy Spirit, to seek the fulfillment of this high calling.

The Sacred Ardor of Femininity

I acknowledge the sacred ardor of set-apart femininity. I understand that to truly love my future husband well, I must love him with the very love of Christ. As Christ loved me and gave Himself for me, I will seek to sacrificially love and serve my future husband, both now and after marriage. Rather than fighting for my own needs and rights, my goal will be to lay my life down on behalf of my spouse. And even if no earthly love story comes my way, it will be my supreme joy and privilege to serve others and wash their feet, doing for others what Christ has done for me. I acknowledge this sacred ardor and commit, by the enabling power of the Holy Spirit, to seek the fulfillment of this high calling.

The Sacred Cultivation of Femininity

I acknowledge the sacred cultivation of set-apart femininity. I realize that the work of God must progress and not stagnate within my soul. I understand that I must wrestle in prayer for the fullness of Christ's work to be made manifest in my life and in the lives of others around me. I will not accept breaches in the walls surrounding my soul, but will seek, by the power of the Holy Spirit, to place brick upon brick until every last access point in my life is sealed off for Christ's glory. I understand that the Almighty must prepare me for the holy work of Christ's kingdom by diminishing my flesh and cultivating His strength and spiritual authority in my life. I acknowledge this sacred cultivation and commit, by the enabling power of the Holy Spirit, to seek the fulfillment of this high calling.

The Sacred Claim on Femininity

I acknowledge the sacred claim on set-apart femininity. Christ's blood has purchased me and is making me whole so that I, like my Messiah, might become broken bread and poured-out wine for this world. Just as the Holy Spirit has a claim on my spirit, soul, and body and is authorized to do with my life as He wills, so too the Holy Spirit has asked me to become willing to allow Him to lend "His claim over me" to the lost in the world, the poor, the orphan, the widow, the blind, the lame, the deaf, the naked, the imprisoned, the outcast, the oppressed, and the lonely—that my life might become bread and drink for them, and that through my willingness to be broken and spilled, they might see, comprehend, and place their trust in the person and glory of God. I acknowledge this sacred claim and commit, by the enabling power of the Holy Spirit, to seek the fulfillment of this high calling.

The Sacred Ceremony

I hereby state that my body and my blood are my God's to spend and that He has both an "intent for" and a "claim on" my feminine existence. I recognize that without the enabling power of God's grace I am incapable of living out this high and holy pattern for femininity and, therefore, such a life and testimony of sacred set-apartness can only be achieved through a constant abiding in Christ's life, love, and strength. Therefore, I hereby beckon the Spirit of God to tax the remotest star and the last grain of sand to assist me with this holiest of endeavors, that by His almighty power I might demonstrate clearly to the world His grand kingdom and His great glory.

Signature   Date

Precious sisters, thank you for joining me on this narrow, rocky path. I am standing beside you in prayer. I am cheering you on in the spiritual realm. Let me leave you with these final words from a few women who changed the world.

> We are made for larger ends than earth can compass. O let us be true to our exalted destiny!
>
> —Catherine Booth
> 1829-1890

> I cannot forsake my faith for freedom.
>
> —Vibia Perpetua
> 181-203

> Lord, let me think no evil, bear all things, hope all things, endure all things. Let me walk in humility and Godly fear before all men and in Thy sight.
>
> —Elizabeth Fry
> 1780-1845

> Comrades, let us be resolute. Let us, by whatever name we are called, be Soldiers, Nazarites, Priests. Some will praise us, some will blame us; let us not care too much about either praise or blame. Let us live looking up, looking on, standing true by the grace of Him who has called us.[4]
>
> —Amy Carmichael
> 1867-1961

Notes

Chapter One: Sacred Intent

1. Dr. Nancy Etcoff and Dr. Susie Orbach, "Only Two Percent of Women Describe Themselves as Beautiful," *Campaignforrealbeauty/Dove®* (2004), http://www .campaignforrealbeauty.com/press.asp?section=news&id=110.

2. Lisa DePaulo, "Adriana Lima: Our Favorite…Virgin?" *Men.style.com,* http://men .style.com/gq/features/full?id=content_4255.

3. Jackie Pullenger, *Releasing the Oppressed,* audiotapes from Vineyard Christian Fellowship in Fort Collins, Colorado.

4. Amy Carmichael, *Gold Cord* (London, England: London Society for Promoting Christian Knowledge, 1947).

5. Rachel Dretzin Goodman and Barak Goodman (producers), *The Lost Children of Rockdale County,* 90-minute documentary (1996), PBS Video, Melbourne, Florida, http://www.pbs.org/wgbh/pages/frontline/shows/georgia/etc/tapes.html.

6. Amy Carmichael, *God's Missionary* (Fort Washington, PA: Christian Literature Crusade, 1998), 34.

7. Edith Deen, *Great Women of the Christian Faith* (Westwood, NJ: Barbour, 1959), 3.

8. Ibid. 164-71.

9. Gladys Aylward, *The Little Woman* (Chicago, IL: Moody Press, 1974).

10. The Voice of the Martyrs, *Hearts of Fire* (Nashville, TN: W Publishing Group, 2003), 109-58.

11. Oswald Chambers, *The Complete Works of Oswald Chambers* (Grand Rapids, MI: Discovery House Publishers, 2000), 850.

Chapter Two: Sacred Design

1. Elisabeth Elliot, *A Chance to Die: The Life and Legacy of Amy Carmichael* (Grand Rapids, MI: Revel, 1987), 37.

2. Leonard Ravenhill, *Testimony,* an audio recording of a personal interview, http:// www.sermonindex.net.

3. Amy Carmichael, *Gold Cord* (London, England: London Society for Promoting Christian Knowledge, 1947), 159-62.

4. John and Stasi Eldredge. *Captivating* (Nashville, TN: Nelson Books, 2005), 6.

5. Oswald Chambers, *The Complete Works of Oswald Chambers* (Grand Rapids, MI: Discovery House Publishers, 2000), 570.

6. John and Stasi Eldredge *Captivating* (Nashville, TN: Nelson Books, 2005), 131-32.

7. Ian Thomas, *The Mystery of Godliness* (Grand Rapids, MI: Zondervan Publishing House, 1964), 162.

8. Oswald Chambers, *The Complete Works of Oswald Chambers* (Grand Rapids, MI: Discovery House Publishers, 2000), 570.

9. Ian Thomas, *The Mystery of Godliness* (Grand Rapids, MI: Zondervan, 1964), 185.

Chapter Three: Sacred Priority

1. Elizabeth Dodds, *Marriage to a Difficult Man* (Philadelphia, PA: The Westminster Press), 17.

Chapter Four: Sacred Decorum

1. Ian Thomas, *The Indwelling Life,* (Sisters, OR: Multnomah Publishers, 2006), 34.

2. Alan Redpath, As quoted in *Why Revival Tarries* by Leonard Ravenhill (Minneapolis, MN: Bethany House, 1987), 56

3. Amy Carmichael, *Gold Cord* (London, England: London Society for Promoting Christian Knowledge, 1947), 3.

4. Amy Carmichael, *God's Missionary* (Fort Washington, PA: Christian Literature Crusade, 1998), 39.

5. Leonard Ravenhill, *The Chapel in the Air* radio interview conducted by David Mains, http://www.sermonindex.net.

6. Amy Carmichael, *God's Missionary* (Fort Washington, PA: Christian Literature Crusade, 1998), 32-33.

7. Joseph Telushkin, *Jewish Literacy* (NY: William Morrow and Co., 1991), 74.

8. Rabbi Shmuley Boteach, *Never Fear Being Hated* adapted from an address by Rabbi Shmuley to his son Mendy in synagogue on Saturday, May 6, 2006, http://www.worldnetdaily.com/news/article.asp?ARTICLE_ID=50199.

9. Leonard Ravenhill, *Why Revival Tarries* (Bloomington, MN: Bethany House Publishers, 1979), 34.

10. Ibid. 35.

11. Henry Blackaby, *Experiencing God* (Nashville, TN: Lifeway Press, 1993), 23.

12. Leonard Ravenhill, *Why Revival Tarries* (Bloomington, MN: Bethany House Publishers, 1979), 34-35.

13. Ibid. 56.

Chapter Five: Sacred Mystique

1. Reprinted by permission of the publisher. Eric and Leslie Ludy, *Meet Mr. Smith* (Nashville, TN: Thomas Nelson Publishers, 2007), 194-98.

Chapter Six: Sacred Cultivation

1. Leonard Ravenhill, *Why Revival Tarries* (Bloomington, MN: Bethany House Publishers, 1979), 71.

2. Dr. and Mrs. Howard Taylor, *Hudson Taylor: The Early Years* (Littleton, CO: OMF International, 2007), 79.

3. Thomas O. Chisholm, lyrics to *Great Is Thy Faithfulness* (Carol Stream, IL: Hope Publishing Company, 1923).

4. Karen Lee-Thorpe, *Waking Up from the Dream of a Lifetime* (Colorado Springs, CO: Navpress, 2005), back cover.

5. Leonard Ravenhill, *Why Revival Tarries* (Bloomington, MN: Bethany House Publishers, 1979), 71.

6. Sparks, T. Austin, *The School of Christ* (Lindale, TX: World Challenge, Inc., 1964), 9.

7. Catherine Booth, As quoted by Edith Deen in *Great Women of the Christian Faith* (Uhrichsville, OH: Barbour Publishing, Inc., 1986), 223.

8. Gladys Aylward (author) and Christine Hunter (contributor), *The Little Woman* (Chicago, IL: Moody Publishers, 1980), 29-30.

9. Amy Carmichael, *Gold Cord* (London, England: London Society for Promoting Christian Knowledge, 1947), 46.

10. Leonard Ravenhill, *Why Revival Tarries* (Bloomington, MN: Bethany House Publishers, 1979), 89.

11. Derek Prince, *Blessing or Curse* (Grand Rapids, MI: Chosen Books, 2006), 30.

12. Samuel Chadwick, As quoted in *Revival Prayer* by Leonard Ravenhill (Minneapolis, MN: Bethany House, 2005), 44.

13. E.M. Bounds, *Complete Words of E.M. Bounds on Prayer* (Grand Rapids, MI: Baker Books, 1990), 41-42.

14. Ibid. 41.

15. E.M. Bounds, As quoted in *Why Revival Tarries* by Leonard Ravenhill (Bloomington, MN: Bethany House Publishers, 1979), 24.

16. Leonard Ravenhill, *Why Revival Tarries* (Bloomington, MN: Bethany House Publishers, 1979), 73.

17. Trevor Yaxley, *William and Catherine* (Minneapolis, MN: Bethany House, 2003), 98-99.

18. Elisabeth Elliot, *A Chance to Die: The Life and Legacy of Amy Carmichael* (Revel, 2005), 91-92.

19. James E. Kiefer, Information found online at http://justus.anglican.org/resources/bio/73.html.

20. Hudson Taylor, *A Retrospect* (London, England: China Inland Mission, 1894), 5.

21. Edward Meyrick Goulburn, As quoted in *Streams in the Desert* by L.B.Cowman (Grand Rapids, MI: Zondervan, 1996), 221.

22. Karen Lee-Thorpe, *Waking Up from the Dream of a Lifetime* (Colorado Springs, CO: Navpress, 2005), back cover.

23. Leonard Ravenhill, *Why Revival Tarries* (Bloomington, MN: Bethany House Publishers, 1979), 25-26.

24. Leonard Ravenhill, *Why Revival Tarries* (Bloomington, MN: Bethany House Publishers, 1979), 85.

25. Amy Carmichael, *Gold Cord* (London, England: London Society for Promoting Christian Knowledge, 1947), 58.

Chapter Seven: Sacred Ardor

1. Reprinted by permission of the publisher. Eric and Leslie Ludy, *When God Writes Your Love Story* (Colorado Springs, CO: Multnomah Publishers, 2004), 247.

2. The Voice of the Martyrs. *Hearts of Fire,* (Nashville, TN: Word Publishing Group, 2003), 109-57.

3. Reprinted by permission of the publisher. Eric and Leslie Ludy, *The First 90 Days of Marriage* (Nashville, TN: W Publishing, 2006), 102-3.]

4. Elisabeth Elliot, *Let Me Be a Woman* (Wheaton, IL: Tyndale House Publishers, 1976), 47.

Chapter Eight: Sacred Claim

1. Jackie Pullenger, *Testimony,* an audio recording of a personal interview, http://www.sermonindex.net.

2. John Eldredge, *Wild at Heart* (Nashville, TN: Nelson Books, 2001), 203.

3. Carolyn Cox and John Marks, *This Immoral Trade* (Grand Rapids, MI: Monarch Books, 2006), 11.

4. Edith Deen, *Great Women of the Christian Faith* (Westwood, NJ: Barbour, 1959), 220.

5. *Becoming "Biblezine"* (Nashville, TN: Thomas Nelson, 2008), back cover.

6. Ian Thomas, *The Mystery of Godliness* (Grand Rapids, MI: Zondervan, 1964), 187.

7. Jackie Pullenger, *Testimony,* an audio recording of a personal interview, http://www.sermonindex.net.

8. Leonard Ravenhill, *Testimony,* an audio recording of a personal interview, http://www.sermonindex.net.

9. Hunger and World Poverty Sources: United Nations World Food Program (WFP), Oxfam, UNICEF as viewed online at http://www.poverty.com.

10. Jackie Pullenger, *Testimony,* an audio recording of a personal interview, http://www.sermonindex.net.

11. Jackie Pullenger, *Releasing the Oppressed,* audiotapes from Vineyard Christian Fellowship in Fort Collins, Colorado.

Chapter Nine: Sacred Ceremony

1. Dr. William Edwin Sangster, As quoted in *Revival Prayer* by Leonard Ravenhill (Minneapolis, MN: Bethany House, 2005), 143.

2. Amy Carmichael, *Gold Cord* (London, England: London Society for Promoting Christian Knowledge, 1947), 161-62.

3. Norman Grubb, *Rees Howells Intercessor* (Fort Washington, PA: Christian Literature Crusade, 1952), 179.

4. Amy Carmichael, *God's Missionary* (Fort Washington, PA: Christian Literature Crusade, 1998), 55.

Wondering where to go from here?
take the next step...

EXCERPT FROM
LESLIE LUDY'S NEW BOOK

Answering the Guy Questions

Coming in Spring 2009

By the time I reached high school I had completely given up on the idea of finding a prince charming.

Most guys I knew hung posters of bikini-clad supermodels on their bedroom walls and carried *Playboy* magazines to school in their backpacks. They implied that any high school girls they dated were merely stand-ins until they finally had the chance to hook up with their *real* fantasy—a Victoria's Secret model or *Playboy* centerfold (conveniently overlooking the fact that they could never snag that kind of woman in the first place). Like countless other girls, I became jaded by the sex-obsessed minds of modern guys. I was plagued by insecurity, knowing that no matter how physically attractive I became, I could never measure up to the culture's impossible standards for feminine sex appeal and thus, I could never really capture the heart of a modern guy.

The extra discouraging wrinkle to the whole saga was that Christian guys didn't seem much different than all the other warped, perverted men of modern times. In fact, my youth pastor Kevin Richards greeted me (and several other girls) each week as we entered the youth room with a sly smile and the question, "So, who's your boyfriend this week?" Even my "Christian" male leader seemed to see girls the way all the other guys did—merely there for the pleasure and enjoyment of men. If we weren't hopping from boyfriend to boyfriend, then Kevin implied that we were abnormal. And if we weren't with guys, we seemed to have very little purpose or value in his eyes.

In my book *Authentic Beauty,* I described a shocking experience I had when I overheard a conversation between three "Christian" guys in the school cafeteria. Though they were clean-cut, church-going guys, I listened in disgust as they lustfully described several girls' bodies (and the sexual acts they desired to do with them) in pornographic detail. Later when I confronted one of the guys (he happened to be an acquaintance of mine who sat behind me in Spanish class) about the depravity of his mind, I was told in a patronizing tone, "This is just the way guys are—get over it."

Though I was discouraged and disgusted by the state of modern masculinity, I was desperately afraid of being unappealing to the opposite sex. Like most other girls my age, I reasoned that being treated like a sex object was better than being disregarded by guys and spending the rest of my life alone. So I began catering to the masculine perversion all around me—dressing seductively to gain male approval, laughing carelessly when guys explored my body in the halls at school, and giving away my heart, emotions, and almost all of my physical purity to one casual meaningless fling after the next. And like most other girls my age, giving in to the dismal standard of modern masculinity left me heartbroken, wounded, and plagued with debilitating insecurity. My feminine heart still longed for prince charming. But my reality screamed that my desire for a noble knight was an immature, idiotic dream that could never come true and that I was destined to end up with a self-focused, egotistical man who would always be lusting after other women even after he had pledged his heart to me.

Popular urban legend states that men think about sex approximately every seven seconds. Though there is no way to prove such a statement, simply being around modern guys seems to validate that rumor as scientific fact. It's a catch-22 when you think about it. The culture sends a clear message to boys from the time that they are old enough to even notice the opposite sex. The message implies that they are not normal unless they are fixated on the female body. It becomes a self-fulfilling prophecy—boys want to be seen as masculine so they eagerly step into the role that society creates for them, becoming sex-obsessed cavemen incapable of seeing women as anything more than pieces of meat to be lustfully devoured. The result is the perverted, sex-addicted version of manhood we see all around us. And in case we ever doubt the severity of the problem, all we need to do is take a look at these startling facts:

- Nearly 28 million guys visit at least one Internet porn site every month.
- The largest group of Internet porn users is made up of boys between the ages of 12 and 17.
- The Internet porn industry generates 12 billion dollars in annual revenue—more than the combined annual revenue of ABC, CBS, and NBC.

Though the Christian men of our culture are supposed to be the ones who will rise above the debased mediocrity around them, they are ensnared by the same warped perspective and sinful sexual vices as the rest of their male counterparts. In fact, the church is literally inundated with pastors, leaders, and Christ-professing men who are enslaved to Internet porn, premarital sex, adulterous affairs, and even homosexuality. According to a 2001 survey of clergy who had Internet access, 51 percent said Internet pornography was a possible tempta-tion, and 37 percent said it was a current struggle (*Christianity Today*, December 2001). And these were just the ones who were being honest when polled!

And even more disturbing is the defeated attitude that we as Chris-tians have taken toward this issue. Not long ago I sat in a pastor's office as he criticized a wife for being "offended" at her husband's pornography addiction. "He's not a pervert or a sex addict," the pastor said. "He's just a normal, red-blooded male. Every guy deals with this, and it's time we stop making men feel ashamed about it."

While I understand the reasoning behind such an attitude, I also believe it is extremely dangerous. Men with sexual addictions should not be mercilessly condemned by the church—as in, "You are a hopeless, disgusting pervert, and God wants nothing to do with you." However, we have swung in the opposite direction, eagerly embracing and even cheering on men in their sex-obsessed state, without expecting them to be set free by the transforming grace of God.

I can't even count the number of young women who have written to me over the past few years, telling me about sexual compromise within their church. Some of them have been sexually assaulted by their youth pastors. Others have engaged in secret affairs with pastors or worship leaders. Still others have been sexually abused by their fathers—men who often were elders, deacons, or leaders in the church.

A young man who just graduated from a Christian college told me, "The problem of sexual perversion is beyond rampant—even in the church. Having just come out of a Christian college, I can tell you categorically that there's not a guy I met who wasn't either struggling with lust or completely given over to it. Many even seemed to take some pride in the fact."

So how are we, as women, supposed to respond to the vast cavern between the righteous standard of Christ and the disturbing reality of modern masculinity? Thus far, we haven't been given the right answer. I have read several books and magazine articles for Christian women that seek to help us live with guys' lust problems in an understanding, non-nagging, non-critical way. "We as women can't possibly understand a man's intense sex drive," they exhort us, "and it's time we stop making them feel like criminals for just doing what comes naturally to them."

Criticism, nagging, or heaping guilt upon men, to be sure, will not help a man battling sex addictions and perversion. But neither will shrugging our shoulders and saying "guys will be guys."

What modern masculinity needs is a serious shot of the *saving, redeeming, transforming, delivering power of Jesus Christ.*

And as women, it's time we realize that we play significant roles in seeing that come about. If you have ever been discouraged, disgusted, depressed, or even defeated by the state of modern masculinity, this book can infuse you with vision, hope, and a practical means of doing something about it.

The problems of modern manhood are not too big for God. He has a huge vision for His men—the very standard of Jesus Christ. And if you are willing, you can be a part of one of the most amazing, God-inspired reformations in history—a radical return of manhood as God intended it to be, in all of its glory, strength, nobility, and honor.

Here's a quick peek at some of the highlights from Leslie's new book:

- Warrior Poet Manhood: *The way modern guys are and the way God wants them to be*
- Unlocking your Feminine Power: *Shaping the course of modern masculinity*
- Code of Conduct: *How to treat guys in everyday life*
- Fairy Tale Love Stories: *The blueprint for a Christ-built relationship*
- Capturing His Heart: *What makes a woman truly beautiful to a Christ-built man?*